China's Reform and Opening-up Drive

The 30 Defining Events of the First 30 Years

Compiled by: *BusinessWatch* magazine
Translated by: Matthew Trueman

新星出版社
NEW STAR PRESS

Compiled by: *BusinessWatch* magazine
Translated by: Matthew Trueman

Publisher: Xie Gang
Editor: Zhang Wei
Book design and layout: zhengmei 正美
Cover design: Lydia Lin

First Edition 2008

China's Reform and Opening-up Drive
The 30 Defining Events of the First 30 Years

ISBN 978-7-80225-541-8
NEW STAR PRESS
Published by NEW STAR PRESS
Longji Building, 67 Jinbao Street, Dongcheng District, Beijing 100005, China
Home Page: http://www.newstarpress.com
E-mail Address: newstar@newstarpress.com

Distributed by China International Book Trading Corporation
35 Chegongzhuang Xilu, Beijing 100044, China
P.O.Box 399, Beijing, China

Printed in the People's Republic of China

Contents

01 The Third Plenary Session of the 11th Central Committee and the Launch of China's Reform and Opening-up Drive /2

02 The Unification of Income Tax Rates for Domestic and Foreign Enterprises /7

03 China's Accession to the WTO /14

04 The Abolition of Agricultural Taxes /19

05 Lenovo's Acquisition of IBM PC /24

06 The *Labor Contract Law* Dispute /29

07 The State Commission for Economic Restructuring: 1982 to 2003 /34

08 Taking the Lead: China's Special Economic Zones /39

09 The "Contract Responsibility System": The Pioneer of China's Reform /45

10 The *Bashan* Steamer Conference /50

11 The "Double-Track Pricing System": From Planning to Market /57

12 The Development of Pudong /65

13 The Scientific Outlook on Development /73

14 Deng Xiaoping's "Southern Tour" /79

15 The Socialist Market Economy: China's New Reform Target /86

Contents

16 *Property Law*: Equal Protection for Public and Private Property /92

17 The Imposition of Individual Income Tax /101

18 Split-share Structure Reform /107

19 Building a Well-off Society in an All-around Way /114

20 The Birth of China's Stock Market /122

21 The Introduction of "Nine Provisions of the State Council" /128

22 Tax Revenue-sharing System Reform /134

23 Thirty Years of SOE Reform /140

24 The Launch of Banking Reform /146

25 China's New Dream: Building a Harmonious Society /152

26 The Non-public Economy: A "Major Component" /158

27 China's "No-devaluation" Pledge /164

28 "Three Represents" and Private Property Protection /171

29 China's "New Countryside" Campaign /178

30 From Regional Revitalization to Coordinated Development /183

1. The Third Plenary Session of the 11th Central Committee and the Launch of China's Reform and Opening-up Drive

From December 18 to 22, 1978, the Third Plenary Session of the 11th Central Committee of the Communist Party of China (CCCPC) was held in Beijing. This plenum is regarded as the starting point of China's "reform and opening-up." The key outcomes of this session were a shift in the Party's work focus towards modernization, and strengthening of the leadership to execute this strategic decision. During the session, the ideological line of "emancipating the mind and seeking truth from facts" was also reaffirmed.

The communique of the Third Plenary Session of the 11th CCCPC placed special emphasis on the importance of economic construction, stating: "We must set out to rectify the erroneous

tendency of being overanxious for success, and the entire Party must pay attention to resolving the severe proportionate imbalance in the national economy. We must adopt a series of new and important measures to adjust the proportions of the national economy, which have fallen into imbalance; and embark on diligently reforming the system of economic management to address its over-concentration of power. On the basis of self-reliance, we must actively develop equal and mutually beneficial economic cooperation with countries around the world; endeavor to adopt the world's advanced technology and equipment; and vigorously strengthen work in science and education that is needed to achieve modernization. These ideologies are the basis upon which the Communist Party of China (CPC) has established the important policy of opening up to the outside world and revitalizing the domestic economy."

The above excerpt was the original declaration of the guiding principle known as "one central task and two basic points." "One

central task" refers to the task of focusing efforts on "developing the productive forces"; the "two basic points" refer to reform and opening-up.

No significant leadership changes were made at the Third Plenary Session of the 11th CCCPC. Although the then 74-year-old Deng Xiaoping was only the third highest ranking leader of the CPC in 1977, he had already gained the support of the majority of people both inside and outside the Party. Furthermore, among Chinese statesmen, only the seemingly undefeatable Deng (who had survived "three ups and three downs" during his political career) was not only unrivaled in terms of experience but also boasted the full range of leadership skills—in Party, administrative and army roles as well as economic construction. At the plenum, Deng's thinking and decision-making, for the first time, played a central and vital role—and had a decisive effect on the historical transformation of Party policy.

Between October 1949 and the convocation of the Third Plenary Session of the 11th CCCPC in December 1978, the Party convened a total of 25 Central Committee plenums. The reason that this particular plenary session was so significant and received so much attention is that it marked a great turning point in the contemporary history of China.

The profound historic significance of this turning point is twofold. First, the plenum witnessed the generational succession of the Party's top leadership, and the dawn of the Deng

Xiaoping era. Second, the strategic decision was made at the plenum to shift the Party's work focus and the public's attention to the socialist modernization drive.

The Third Plenary Session of the 11th CCCPC was, in fact, the second critical turning point in the Party's history. The first such turning point was an enlarged session of the Political Bureau of the CCCPC convened in Zunyi City, Guizhou in January 1935; at the session, Mao Zedong's role as leader of the CPC was established, giving rise to the first generation of Party leadership (headed by Mao). The second such turning point, as mentioned, was the Third Plenary Session of the 11th CCCPC, convened in Beijing in December 1978; it was at this plenum that Deng Xiaoping's role as Party leader was confirmed, spawning the second generation of CPC leadership (with Deng at its core).

Indeed, the historic significance of the Third Plenary Session of the 11th CCCPC may be even greater when viewed across China's entire modern history. In this historical sense, the plenum symbolized the rejuvenation of the Chinese nation: the end of China's movement (that began in 1840) to "save itself from extinction," and the dawn of its landmark mission to become a strong and prosperous nation.

2. The Unification of Income Tax Rates for Domestic and Foreign Enterprises

On March 16, 2007, *Enterprise Income Tax Law of the People's Republic of China (Draft)* was voted through at the Fifth Session of the 10th National People's Congress (NPC, China's top legislature). On March 19, Chinese president Hu Jintao signed "Presidential Order No. 63," formally promulgating *Enterprise Income Tax Law of the People's Republic of China* (hereafter *Enterprise Income Tax Law*). With the resultant unification of income tax laws for domestic- and foreign-funded enterprises, the era of "super-national treatment" for FFEs reached its finale.

The new *Enterprise Income Tax Law*, which comprises eight chapters and 60 articles, took effect on January 1, 2008. The law fol-

lows common international practices, embodying "four unifications": unification of the enterprise income tax laws applicable to domestic- and foreign-funded enterprises; unification and appropriate reduction of enterprise income tax rates; unification and standardization of pre-tax deduction methods and standards; and unification of preferential tax policies.

The new *Enterprise Income Tax Law* stipulates that enterprises and other income-earning organizations inside the territory of China are liable to pay business income taxes. The law establishes a unified tax rate of 25 percent for both domestic- and foreign-funded enterprises, eight percentage points lower than the original rate. In this way, the new tax law resolves the issues of different tax treatment for domestic and foreign enterprises and the large discrepancy between their respective tax burdens. In addition, since the newly adjusted tax rate of 25 percent is lower than the average global rate as well as those of neighboring countries, it still remains an attractive incentive to foreign enterprises.

Previously, China had practised a "double-track system" of en-

terprise income taxation. Under this system, foreign-funded enterprises were subject to the *Income Tax Law of the People's Republic of China for Enterprises with Foreign Investment and Foreign Enterprises*, passed at the Fourth Session of the Seventh NPC in 1991; while domestic-funded enterprises were governed by the *Provisional Regulations of the People's Republic of China on Enterprise Income Tax*, issued by the State Council in 1993. Although the nominal income tax rate for both domestic- and foreign-funded enterprises was 33 percent, in practice the actual average tax burden of domestic-funded enterprises was about 25 percent, while that of foreign-funded enterprises was only around 15 percent. For over 20 years after China opened up to the outside world, this "supernational treatment" granted to foreign-funded enterprises attracted large amounts of foreign direct investment, helped China to solve its employment problem, and played an important role in enabling China to rapidly upgrade its manufacturing capabilities and management skills. At the same time, however, it resulted in domestic enterprises being placed in a disadvantageous position in competing with foreign-funded enterprises. This inequity prompted growing calls for the unification of China's two sets of enterprise income tax laws, especially after China's accession to the World Trade Organization (WTO).

The new *Enterprise Income Tax Law* includes a series of preferential tax policies designed to promote the upgrade of China's industrial structure and the harmonious development of regional economies, yielding a new preferential tax structure centered on industry-based policies, supported by region-specific policies, and conducive to social progress. The new tax policies are especially favorable to high-tech enterprises as well as enterprises investing in environmental protection. Preferential tax treatment for investment in infrastructure construction, farming, forestry, animal husbandry and fishery is maintained under the new law, while the policy of direct tax reduction or exemption is replaced by indirect tax breaks. Although the new law abolishes region-specific preferential tax policies for special economic zones and economic development zones, a transition period is provided for foreign-funded enterprises already established in special economic zones, Pudong New Area, or any of the regions covered by China's Western Development initiative.

The *Enterprise Income Tax Law* also introduces the concept of resident and non-resident enterprises, following the common international practice of using place of registration and place of effective management as evaluative criteria. This logical categorization supplants the irrational framework under which enterprise income tax was determined based on the nature of ownership or source of capital of the enterprise. Resident enterprises assume unlimited tax liability and must pay tax in China on all earnings derived from China and abroad. Non-resident enterprises assume limited tax liability and must pay tax in China only on income derived from China. According to the new law, any non-resident enterprise with no office or establishment inside China and any non-resident enterprise with income that bears no practical connection to its institution or establishment inside China shall pay

enterprise income tax on any income derived from China at a tax rate of 20 percent.

The reform path of China's enterprise income tax scheme embodies the development course of the country's economic system as a whole. During the early stages of reform and opening-up, China was in urgent need of large amounts of foreign capital, advanced production technology and management experience. Thus was born the era of preferential tax policies for foreign-funded enterprises. With the development of the market economy—especially after the transition period following China's accession to the WTO had ended—the differential tax system, which was not only opposed by public opinion but also ran counter to the spirit of fair trade advocated by the WTO, was duly abrogated, facilitating the establishment of a unified, standardized market environment conducive to fair competition. The new tax law provides a more transparent, stable and predictable tax system for all market participants.

The unification of China's enterprise income tax for domestic- and foreign-funded enterprises embodies not only the formation of a "fair competition" tax environment, but also a shift in the

focus of preferential tax policies from foreign investment attraction to industrial structure optimization. This is consistent with China's modern financial and tax ideology of promoting social equity and optimizing the industrial structure through financial and taxation measures.

The new preferential tax policies reflect a shift from region-based preferences to industry-specific preferences. The abolishment of the "special zone" status or "special privileges" previously afforded to some regions will facilitate a more equitable balance in regional benefits. This will also play an important role in rectifying local governments' long-term habit of intervening in economic life in pursuit of financial gain. In addition, decreasing the overall tax burden on enterprises will directly alter the trend of recent years, whereby social distribution was excessively tilted towards government and the rate of tax revenue growth far exceeded that of GDP growth. In a deeper sense, then, the reform of China's enterprise income tax system is an institutional affirmation of the transformation of China's society and the transition of its economic system.

3. China's Accession to the WTO

On November 10, 2001, the Resolution on China's Accession to the World Trade Organization was passed at the Fourth Ministerial Conference of the WTO. Thirty days later, on December 11, China officially became a member of the WTO.

By then, it had been over 15 years since China applied to restore its status as a contracting party to the General Agreement on Tariffs and Trade (GATT) in July 1986. During 15 years of negotiations for GATT status resumption and WTO accession, China persevered through arduous challenges and a whirlwind of ups and downs. No other country seeking admission to the WTO experienced as many twists and turns as China did during its accession quest. In the words of Long Yongtu, China's chief WTO negotiator, the process was one in which "black-haired persons talked (long

enough) to become white-haired."

Between 1999 and 2001, China made a massive and unprecedented overhaul of its domestic laws and regulations in order to accommodate the requirements for WTO accession. In total, China revised or abolished over 2,000 laws, regulations and decrees that had conflicted with WTO rules as part of active efforts to align with general WTO rules.

For China, as a developing country and new WTO member, fulfilling its accession commitment—to implement further tariff reductions and increase market openness—would not be a cakewalk. At the time, some people even doubted whether China was capable of abiding by its accession promises. The fact, however, is that China's overall tariff level dropped from almost 40 percent in the early 1990s to 9.9 percent in 2005 (according to data published by the WTO), while non-tariff measures were annulled as of January 1, 2005. In addition, finance, insurance, telecommunications, ocean shipping, audio and video distribution, tourism and other industries and sectors were further opened to the outside world; obligations to open China's service trade market were fulfilled; and intellectual property protection was greatly strengthened. With respect to investment, China amended its *Catalogue for the Guidance of Foreign Investment Industries* in 2004 to fully accord with China's accession promises. On November 15, 2006, China issued *Regulations on the Administration of Foreign-funded Banks*, which set out that, as of December 11, 2006, all remaining restrictions on foreign-funded banks' domestic renminbi (RMB) services would be lifted.

China's WTO accession reflects both the world's acceptance of China and China's integration into the world. With its entry into the WTO, China formally entered the international division-of-labor system and the world trade system, enabling China to fully utilize its comparative advantages and become an increasingly domi-

nant force in the global economic order. Furthermore, since its accession to the WTO, China has not only reaped the economic benefits of globalization, but has also continued to deepen its own reforms as it integrates into the world market.

In the first five years following its WTO accession, China's foreign trade surged at an average annual rate of more than 30 percent—far higher than the average growth rate of world trade during the same period. In 2007, the total value of China's imports and exports climbed above US$2 trillion, ranking third in the world, with the country's exports ranking second. For all intents and purposes, China had become a major player in world trade.

China's huge market size, low labor costs, superior infrastructural environment and stable political and economic conditions have combined to make China an ideal investment destination for multinational companies, resulting in large influxes of foreign direct investment. Foreign companies coming to China have not only made substantial returns on their investments, but have also brought with them opportunities for economic growth and new employment opportunities. The transformation of China's economy is embodied in every aspect of Chinese citizens' lives—from ever-cheaper cars to higher-level banking services. Indeed, entry into the WTO has made China one of the world's few beneficiaries of economic globalization.

On the other hand, WTO accession also meant that China had merged into the capital system of Western developed nations and accepted the regulatory system of global governance. The WTO, however, constitutes an arena not only for cooperation but for competition as well. Many Chinese people initially believed that, after WTO entry, the "unequal treatment" previously imposed on China would naturally be eradicated, and that China would enjoy free-trade privileges in exchange for the complete opening-up of its market. Following China's accession, however, the emergence of a new series of problems—ranging from China's "market economy" status to trade quotas—made it apparent to the Chinese that the WTO was in no way a "free-trade paradise"; one after another, Western countries that had waved the banner of free trade began to raise the level of trade protection barriers under domestic pressure.

The Sino-American and Sino-European textile trade disputes that broke out in 2005 are reflective of such barriers. After WTO

accession, anti-dumping investigations against China increased rapidly, and China became the target of almost one out of every three cases worldwide. Meanwhile, other countries' belief that China was a "non-market economy" led to higher punitive taxes on Chinese exports. Among all the WTO member nations, China has been the only one to face these kinds of discriminatory treatment. As foreign trade continues to surge, China has entered a period of increased trade friction. In order to secure an equal status and greater influence in the world economy, China must learn to utilize, and even participate directly in transforming and formulating, the rules of the game.

Finally, WTO accession represents a paradigm shift: the first complete connection between the Chinese and world markets. On a deeper level, integration into the global regulatory system has impelled China to seek a voice in shaping world trade rules to eliminate inequitable treatment against it and other WTO newcomers. Indeed, admission to the WTO has afforded China a much greater say in negotiations on wide-ranging issues, including the formulation of trade regulations. As a large and developing country, China requires the kind of multilateral and rule-based international trade system epitomized by the WTO. As for the future of global economic trade, China is not only a "system architect," but also a leader in enhancing equity and equality.

4. The Abolition of Agricultural Taxes

On December 29, 2005, the Standing Committee of the 10th NPC passed a resolution to annul *Regulations of the People's Republic of China on Agricultural Tax*, effective January 1, 2006. With this decision, China's 2,600-year-old agricultural tax was officially relegated to the annals of history.

Regulations of the People's Republic of China on Agricultural Tax was adopted and came into effect at the 96th Meeting of the Standing Committee of the First NPC on June 3, 1958. In 1983, in accordance with *Regulations on Agricultural Tax*, the State Council issued *Some Provisions on the Imposition of Agricultural Tax on Income from Agriculture and Forestry Specialty Products* and began to levy agricultural tax on agriculture and forestry specialty products. In 1985, the system of unified purchasing of farm produce by the state according to fixed quotas was abolished. Correspondingly, the form of agricultural tax was also changed from the imposition of grain levies to the collection of a sum of money based on the "reverse ratio of 3:7" (i.e., 30 percent of the price component was the price formerly set for state purchases of grain, while the remaining 70 percent was based on a higher purchase price for grain in excess of the production quota). In addition to achieving this conversion from "tax in kind" to "tax in money," the new agricultural tax also introduced a variety of new preferential tax policies.

After the People's Republic of China came into being, agricultural tax served as an important source of national finance for many years, once accounting for 39 percent of total state revenues. With the development of industrialization, however, China has experienced significant social and economic changes. The value of agricultural tax as a percentage of China's total fiscal revenue stood at 5.5 percent in 1979 and dropped to a mere 1 percent by 2004, reflecting a continuing downward trend.

Since the turn of the millennium, when China's industrializa-

tion entered its middle stages, a variety of agriculture-related problems—such as low agricultural efficiency, low farmer incomes, and increasing agricultural-industrial and rural-urban disparities—have intensified. By the early years of the 21st century, China's "three-dimensional rural problem" (agriculture, farmers, and rural areas) had become the weakest link in the state's social and economic development. At the Fourth Plenary Session of the 16th CCCPC, General Secretary Hu Jintao noted that, as China's industrialization had reached an intermediate stage, the time had come for adopting the approach of "industry nurturing agriculture" and "cities supporting the countryside." This approach, he noted, would facilitate the coordinated development of industry and agriculture and of urban and rural areas. These remarks were made in 2004. The achievements that, by then, had already been made—from implementation of rural tax reform (the goal of which was to ease the burden of farmers by reforming the agricultural tax system and annulling the "three deductions" [for public reserve funds, public welfare funds, and management fees], "five charges" [charges for rural education, family planning, militia training, rural road construction, and subsidies to entitled groups] and other non-tax fees) to the complete abolition of agricultural tax—mark an important milestone in China's agricultural transformation.

On March 15, 2004, Premier Wen Jiabao delivered a government work report to the Second Session of the 10th NPC, stating: "Starting this year, the agricultural tax rate shall be reduced by at least 1 percent per year on average. Agricultural taxes shall be rescinded within five years." In April of the same year, the central government announced pilot reform policies to cut agricultural taxation; agricultural tax was exempted in the provinces of Heilongjiang and Jilin, and the tax rate was reduced for the other 11 major grain-producing provinces. By 2005, 28 provinces and autonomous regions had exempted agricultural tax (Tibet, which had never levied agricultural tax, was not among them), while the agricultural tax rates of Hebei, Shandong and Yunnan provinces were lowered to less than 2 percent at the central government's request. On December 29, 2005, as the Standing Committee of the 10th NPC voted to rescind *Regulations on Agricultural Tax*, the farmer-friendly policy of agricultural tax exemption was formally promulgated into law. China's plan to rescind agricultural taxes was thus completed three years ahead of schedule.

The abolition of China's agricultural tax was a fundamental move that has benefited every Chinese peasant household. In the aggregate, China's 800 million farmers have been freed from

paying about 50 billion yuan per year, an average per-capita tax reduction of 65 yuan—equivalent to 2.2 percent of rural residents' average per-capita net income of 2,936 yuan (2004 data). The abolition of agricultural taxes also means the elimination of a platform on which other fees and taxes were once able to "hitch a ride," enabling policies aimed at easing the tax burden of farmers to realize their full effect. Moreover, there are very few countries in the world that still impose taxes on the agricultural sector, and most developed countries provide agricultural subsidies. With the end of China's post-WTO-accession transition period and the deepening of market-oriented reforms, the Chinese agricultural industry faces serious challenges. China's revocation of agricultural taxes—and the resultant decrease in farmers' production costs—helps to meet these challenges by creating a basis for China's agro-products to compete equally in the global market and, ultimately, raising the international competitiveness of Chinese agriculture.

5. Lenovo's Acquisition of IBM PC

"What would the world be like if mankind lost its imagination?" This is a translation of the famous advertising slogan of China's Lenovo Corporation. In China, Lenovo is known as *Lianxiang*, which, in the Chinese language, means "associative thinking" or "imagination." Indeed, this symbolic enterprise—which was founded in 1984 in a reception room at the Chinese Academy of Sciences' Institute of Computing Technology and today occupies center stage of the world PC arena—has never lacked imagination.

On December 8, 2004, the news that Lenovo had acquired IBM's global PC business for US$1.25 billion caused a sensation throughout the business world. In accordance with the agreement signed

by the two parties, Lenovo paid IBM US$650 million in cash and $US600 million in Lenovo Group shares (based on the closing price on the last day of trading prior to the acquisition announcement), and also assumed US$500 million in the debt of IBM's PC division. In 2003, IBM's PC sales generated approximately US$12 billion in revenues. Following the 2004 buyout, Lenovo's PC business ranked third in the world.

This historic takeover not only created the third largest PC manufacturer in the world, but also vaulted Lenovo to the status of a bona fide multinational corporation. Lenovo Group moved its corporate headquarters from Beijing to New York and appointed IBM's Stephen Ward as CEO. Yang Yuanqing, Lenovo's former President and CEO, was named Chairman of the Board of the post-acquisition Lenovo, while Lenovo founder Liu Chuanzhi retired to a behind-the-scenes role.

With IBM's supreme status, Lenovo would no doubt be able to greatly enhance its own brand worldwide. After the transaction, sales derived from the overseas market became an important component of Lenovo's total revenue, jumping from less than 2 percent to 81 percent. Lenovo has become a veritably "internationalized" company.

This major acquisition, which Liu Chuanzhi called "a towering feat," attracted attention from around the globe. The *Wall Street Journal* praised the deal as "a milestone in China's integration in world business" and called it "the dawn of a new era in China's M&A market." *BusinessWeek* magazine wrote: "This is a strange moment. An icon of Western capitalism is marrying a company that's partly owned by the Chinese government." Some industry

insiders, however, believed Lenovo's move to be a huge gamble with little chance of winning. In an interview given to the *Financial Times*, Michael Dell, founder of Dell, Inc., said rhetorically: "When was the last time you saw a successful acquisition or merger in the computer industry?"

While opinions on the transaction varied widely—from optimistic to cautious to hopeless—all observers would have been hard pressed to find any similar cases. Even though ambitious Chinese firms, in recent years, had already set off a wave of acquisitions and attracted widespread media attention, rarely if ever was the acquisition target a bigger and more developed Western company as it was in Lenovo's case. For Lenovo, the size of the deal itself was enough to greatly boost the company's global market position; and for other Chinese firms with a strong impulse to expand overseas, the complexity of the Lenovo-IBM deal provided them with an operational and inspirational standard. In this sense, the internationalization of Lenovo is of landmark significance for Chinese enterprises entering the era of global integration. As Jiang Ruxiang, president of Zion Management Consulting Company, notes: "Even if (Lenovo's acquisition) is a mistake, it is a great mistake. That is the value of the revolutionary martyr."

China's accession to the WTO in 2001 set off the integration and expansion of Chinese enterprises into the global market. From that point forward, they would have no choice but to face the all-out competition and market dominance of foreign giants. Noting that, even in the domestic market, the threat of international com-

petition looms large, Yang Yuanqing remarked: "If Lenovo stays huddling up in [China], there is a 100 percent chance that the company will meet its own demise within five years."

In fact, Lenovo was not alone in its plight. At around the same time, Haier, TCL, Founder Technology and other major Chinese IT firms had all experienced marked slowdowns in growth. These non-resource-based companies, which relied on market opportunities to grow and develop, found themselves up against the wall. In order to extricate themselves from this predicament, they would be forced to "shift gears"; only by stepping into the global market could China's enterprises enhance their external market share and refine their strategic thinking. Even though it was—and still is—well-known that globalization is a rough road filled with twists and turns, the young and tenacious Yang Yuanqing managed to convince Liu Chuanzhi and Lenovo Group's board of directors that venturing overseas was the only way forward. With this decision, Lenovo set out boldly on a road of no return.

Lenovo's decision was not unique; other Chinese mega-firms, too, had kept a close watch on overseas M&A targets before "taking the plunge"—under equally intense media spotlight, of course—to globalize their operations. Unlike Lenovo, however, each of these attempts ended in failure and disappointment. China's TCL Corporation, for example, set up a high-priced joint venture with the French firm Thomson SA in 2004, but was forced to end the

partnership only two years later. In 2005, a bid by China National Offshore Oil Corporation (CNOOC) to acquire US-based Unocal Corporation for US$18.5 billion also ended in defeat. Nevertheless, regardless of the transaction's final outcome—whether it was the failures of TCL and CNOOC or the success of Lenovo—these intrepid attempts at global expansion symbolize the true beginning of the internationalization of corporate China.

In a report issued by the World Bank in April 2008, China was ranked as the second largest economy in the world. Yet in spite of this macroeconomic prowess, there are still very few Chinese companies that boast a global business network and global brand awareness; similarly, with respect to branding, R&D, management and earnings, most Chinese firms still lag behind the world-class enterprises of developed countries. Nevertheless, it is almost certain that more and more Chinese companies will continue to follow in Lenovo's footsteps and venture onto foreign soil. For them, Lenovo's overseas acquisition and unremitting efforts toward internationalization offer invaluable experience and lessons on how to survive and develop in the context of globalization.

6. The Labor Contract Law Dispute

For the entire working population of China, 2007 can be considered a significant turning point.

On June 29 of that year, the Standing Committee of the 10th NPC passed, by an overwhelming vote, the *Labor Contract Law of the People's Republic of China* (hereafter *Labor Contract Law*). The passage of this law marked the first time that the concepts of the regulation of employers and protection of labor were publicly and resolutely addressed by the Chinese government. Since formally taking effect on January 1, 2008, *Labor Contract Law* has received the public's enthusiastic response, becoming a symbol of Chinese labor policy and of the future direction of the Chinese labor market.

Labor Contract Law is an important law that affects the vital interests of all Chinese citizens, and its formation involved levels of public participation and legislative prudence rare in China's legislative history. The law was drafted and submitted for a first reading on December 24, 2005. Three months later, on March 20, 2006, the NPC Standing Committee published the first draft in its entirety and began soliciting opinions from the public. By April 20, the final day of the solicitation period, the government had received some 200,000 comments from the public—including both employers and employees alike.

The reason for these active "lobbying" efforts by employers and workers was the unavoidable gap between their respective interests. The legislative objective of *Labor Contract Law*, therefore, was to create a unified and equitable law that would settle this "gap of interests" through balanced compromise and that would facilitate harmonious and stable labor relations. The *Labor Law of the People's Republic of China*, enacted in 1994, served as the legislative basis for *Labor Contract Law*.

During the more than 10 years since its inception, the labor contract system established by *Labor Law* had played an important role in protecting the rights and interests of laborers. Nevertheless, the legal framework and policy system provided by *Labor Law* was

insufficient to ensure the equal status of laborers and employers and made the dominant position of employers and enterprises relative to workers difficult to dislodge. Labor contracts lacked binding force and workers' interests lacked a stable guarantee. These shortcomings are best illustrated by the fact that, while China's economy was achieving high and sustained growth, the modest growth rate of workers' wages and salaries paled in comparison to the snowballing growth in the remuneration of employers. Workers' earnings even showed a declining trend in certain regions and industries.

Indeed, the majority of China's ordinary working citizens had been unable to fully reap the benefits of increased wealth generated through China's reform and opening-up. This fact, however, was by no means overlooked by Chinese policymakers. The report to the 17th National Congress of the CPC, made by CCCPC General Secretary Hu Jintao in October 2007, included a long statement on the issue of income distribution system reform, noting: "A proper balance must be struck between efficiency and equity in both primary distribution and redistribution, with particular emphasis on equity in redistribution." As can be seen, the term "equity" figures prominently in this statement.

This statement is regarded as an important adjustment to China's path of economic and social development. Prior thereto, the notion of "letting some people become rich first" had been one of the main features that penetrated the reform of China's economic system for over 20 years; similarly, the principle of "giving priority to efficiency with due consideration to fairness" had continuously been the guiding philosophy of policymakers. In contrast, the report to the 17th National Congress stated: "We will gradually increase the share of personal income in the distribution of national income, and raise that of work remuneration in primary distribution. Vigorous efforts will be made to raise the income of low-income groups, gradually increase poverty-alleviation aid and the minimum wage, and set up a mechanism of regular pay increases for enterprise employees and a mechanism for guaranteeing payment of their salaries."

In addition to this report to the 17th National Congress, 2007 and 2008 also witnessed the introduction of *Labor Contract Law* and a series of supporting policies, symbolizing the onset of a shift in China's labor and employment policies to the benefit of workers. According to the provisions of *Labor Contract Law*, enterprises can no longer dismiss employees at will; with respect to the signing of employment contracts, the new law also introduces the concept of the "open-ended" employment contract. To a large extent, these provisions are designed to protect the rights and interests of employees by restricting enterprises' rights to terminate workers and increasing the costs of doing so. The "Legal Liability" chapter of *Labor Contract Law* contains a total of 16 articles, 13 and a half of which focus on employer obligations; this high degree of legal liability on the part of employers is also of clear advantage to workers.

7. The State Commission for Economic Restructuring: 1982 to 2003

1982 was a year in which the State Council decided to "clean house" and streamline its affiliate agencies; the total number of ministries and commissions was reduced from 52 to 41. On March 8 of that year, however, the Fifth NPC passed a resolution to establish a new agency—the State Commission for Economic Restructuring (SCER). By this time, three years into China's reform and opening-up drive, policymakers realized that only an independent, neutral and power-wielding agency entrusted with formulating and implementing reform policies could navigate through the "labyrinth" of departmental and local interests to carry forward China's reform efforts. At the same time, the SCER also provided China's reform leaders with a think tank distinct from the bureaucratic agencies of the centrally planned economic

environment, enabling maximal efficiency in the decision-making process while remodeling the interest structure of bureaucratic agencies under the old system.

According to its definition at the time, the SCER, a constituent of the State Council, was a comprehensive and specialized institution engaged in researching, coordinating and guiding China's economic restructuring. Its main functions and duties were as follows:

To comprehensively research the relationships between economic restructuring and economic development, scientific and technological advancement and openness to the outside world; to study the relationship between urban and rural reform; to provide solutions and suggestions;

To organize the efforts of the appropriate departments and regions in drafting a medium- and long-term plan and a comprehensive annual implementation plan for national economic restructuring;

To provide guidance to the appropriate departments and regions in formulating economic restructuring plans;

To provide guidance to regions, departments, industries and enterprises in carrying out economic restructuring pilot projects; to organize and promote experimental zones for reform and opening-up and pilot projects for comprehensive urban reform; and to plan, organize and guide the training of economic restructuring and enterprise management programs.

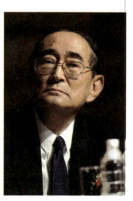

On May 21, 1982, the SCER was officially established on the foundation of the former System Reform Office of the State Council. The SCER was given the primary responsibilities of drafting an overall plan for economic restructuring and researching, planning and guiding the work of restructuring the national economy.

In the years that followed, the SCER was able to recruit large numbers of outstanding individuals, gaining a solid and widespread

reputation and becoming an important driving force for reform. For a time, the SCER even outmatched the State Planning Commission and the State Economic Commission in terms of power and influence. As the SCER was a new agency with no vested interests in the planned economy, it was extremely resolute in pursuing reform. With respect to policy formulation, too, the SCER became an important constraint on other government departments.

In the early years following the establishment of the SCER, the most active institution was the Chinese Economic System Reform Research Institute (CESRRI), a subordinate body of the SCER. CESRRI was a think tank that engaged in direct and frequent dialogue with China's policymakers. It not only served to provide policymakers with innovative reform ideas, but also functioned as a conduit for young economists to advance their reform suggestions to higher levels of authority.

In early-1985, Gao Shangquan, vice-director of the SCER, led the formation of CESRRI and staffed it with relatively young employees. Chen Yizi and Wang Xiaoqiang, both of the Institute of Agricultural Economics' Rural Development Study Group, were respectively appointed as director and deputy director of CESRRI. Soon, the membership of this up-and-coming research institute included almost every young to middle-aged Chinese economist dedicated to reform.

In spite of lacking refined theories, these ambitious economic scholars undertook focused research on urban structural reform and contributed to numerous innovative policies. These policies included the factory director responsibility system; the double-track pricing system; the gradient development strategy for China's central, eastern and western regions; the strategy of opening up the eastern coast; the strategy of having "both ends outside" (i.e., having both supplies and markets outside the domestic economy)

and of importing and exporting on a large scale; the policy of opening up western China; and strategies to address institutional problems in Wenzhou, Zhejiang Province. Furthermore, the work of these economists included not only theoretical analysis, but also specific operating procedures and operating plans. Later, they even became directly involved in the reform of China's political system.

In 1990, however, CESRRI merged with the Economic Management Research Institute to create the Research Institute for

Economic Restructuring and Management. Subsequently, the majority of CESRRI's former members went their own separate ways; some of them went into business on their own, some were hired by other research institutions, and others went overseas to further their education.

Meanwhile, the influence of the SCER on China's reforms weakened significantly and its important ability to constrain departments with vested interests was declining. In March 1998, the State Council initiated the largest scale institutional reform since the founding of the PRC in 1949. The SCER was downgraded to a bureau directly under the State Council and renamed as the "State Council Office for Economic Restructuring." The former SCER's function of organizing and formulating integrated economic laws and regulations for enterprises was handed over to the Legislative Affairs Office of the State Council (LAOSC) and the State Economic and Trade Commission (SETC); the functions of organizing pilot projects for modern enterprise systems and of examining and approving the restructuring of "central enterprises" (i.e., large-scale state-owned enterprises, or SOEs for short, under the direct management of the central government) as limited liability companies were handed over to the SETC; and the function of directing and coordinating comprehensive pilot projects for local reform was transferred to the respective local governments.

In 2003, the State Council Office for Economic Restructuring was disbanded and absorbed into the National Development and Reform Commission.

8. Taking the Lead: China's Special Economic Zones

Initially conceived through the political wisdom of Chinese policymakers, the "special economic zone" (SEZ) is, today, an innovative policy actively studied and implemented by BRIC (Brazil, Russia, India and China), VISTA (Vietnam, Indonesia, South Africa, Turkey and Argentina) and other late-developing nations. SEZs can be considered a new model of international free trade zone. The goal of the SEZ is to promote the economic and technological development of the host country by creating a favorable investment environment, encouraging foreign investment, introducing advanced technology and scientific management methods, and providing tariff concessions and other preferential measures.

The idea of creating special economic zones began in November 1977 during an inspection tour by Deng Xiaoping (then Vice Pre-

mier of the State Council) to Guangdong. At the time, border security forces were having difficulty controlling the increasingly severe problem of people fleeing from Shenzhen to Hong Kong. When Guangdong's authorities presented this "virulent political issue" to Deng, he replied: "This is the problem of our policies. This is not a matter that can be handled by the border security forces."

While many people present at the time puzzled over these words, Wu Nansheng (then secretary of the Guangdong CPC Provincial Committee, and a key figure in Guangdong's later SEZ reforms) was able to read between the lines and extract Deng's implied meaning: "The direction in which border residents flee depends on which place is more attractive. The most fundamental way to curb illegal emigration is to develop the productive forces and truly improve people's living standards."

In January 1979, while conducting research in Shantou, Guangdong Province, Wu Nansheng learned of the concepts of export processing zones and free ports, which had been adopted in Singapore, Hong Kong and Taiwan. This led to Wu's idea of turning Shantou into an export processing zone. Around the same time, Guangdong's Bao'an County also made the suggestion of turning Shenzhen into an export base. Inspired by these ideas, the Guangdong CPC Provincial Committee introduced the first prototype of China's special economic zone—the "trade cooperation zone."

In April of the same year, Guangdong submitted its tentative plan to Beijing and received the approval and encouragement of top central government leaders. Agreeable to the idea of allowing Guangdong to get a "head start," Deng Xiaoping exclaimed: "Let's call it a 'special zone!' The Shaanxi-Gansu-Ningxia Border Region

was a special zone."

On May 5, the Guangdong Provincial CPC Committee went a step further by drafting *Initial Conception of the Pilot Project for Shenzhen, Zhuhai and Shantou Special Export Zones (First Draft)*. This 1,500-word document not only was the first tentative scheme for establishing special zones, but also marked the first time that the term *tequ* ("special zone") appeared in an official document.

On July 15, the CPC Central Committee and State Council issued "Central Document No. 50 (1979)," which approved the provincial Party committee reports of Guangdong and Fujian. The central government decided to implement "special policies and flexible measures" in both Guangdong and Fujian, allowing both provinces to "take the lead" and develop their economies as quickly as possible. The document further stated that "special export zones" should be set up in Shenzhen, Zhuhai, Shantou and Xiamen, and specified the sequential order: "Special export zones can first be set up in Shenzhen and Zhuhai on a pilot basis. After experience has been gained, the establishment of special export zones in Shantou and Xiamen can be considered."

According to the tentative plan of Guangdong Province, a special zone would not merely be a production base, but also a "testing ground" and a "window." Through this window, China would be able to observe the development and transformation of the economy, science and technology, and market supply and demand of the outside world; introduce, learn and domestically propagate the advanced technology and management experience of other

countries; and provide useful experience from which the entire country could learn and benefit. Finally, a special zone would also serve as a large "school" in which to cultivate skilled individuals and transfer them to other parts of China.

Based on the above considerations, and after considering over a dozen alternatives (including "free processing zone," "export processing zone," "border processing zone" and "special export zone"), the term "special economic zone" (*jingji tequ*) was finally selected as the official designation for these newly distinguished regions. On August 26, 1980, Ye Jianying, chairman of the NPC Standing Committee, presided over the 15th Meeting of the Standing Committee of the Fifth NPC. At the meeting, Jiang Zemin, then vice director of the State Import-Export Commission, delivered a presentation on the proposed *Regulations on Special Zones* and related matters on the establishment of special zones. That same day, *Regulations on Special Zones* was passed by the Standing Committee of the Fifth NPC, making August 26 the "birthday" of China's special economic zones.

Over the past 30 years, SEZs have become one of the most important and successful components of China's reform and opening-up experience that can be shared with the world—especially the world economy. Over time, SEZs have gradually formed a set of unique operating rules. In brief, an SEZ is a specified geographi-

cal region (in a particular country), in which the policies governing foreign economic activities are more open and flexible than those of other regions in the same country. An SEZ possesses several key features: it utilizes foreign capital as its primary source of economic development funds; its economic activities are regulated primarily by the market; it provides special privileges and benefits to foreigners coming to invest; and it is granted a fairly high degree of economic autonomy by the government.

In China, SEZs are regions in which the Chinese government implements special policies and allows foreign companies and individuals, overseas Chinese, and Hong Kong and Macau compatriots to engage in investment activities. China's SEZs offer foreign investors preferential conditions in several respects, including: the import of business equipment, raw materials and components as well as the export of products; corporate income tax rates and

tax reductions; foreign exchange settlement and the remittance of profits; land use; and entry/exit and residence procedures for foreign businesspeople and their relatives.

In fact, SEZs have become an exemplar of China's economic reforms, driving and spurring on the development of other regions. In 1988, for example, the island of Hainan was separated from Guangdong Province—to become Hainan Province—and established as China's fifth and largest SEZ. Soon, every province, municipality and autonomous region in China began to imitate the SEZ model and establish "economic development zones" in their respective jurisdictions. This approach—of stimulating reform within the system by setting up new variants outside the system—became one of the core concepts of China's later reforms.

During this period, multiple factors—including its proactive efforts in implementing the "emancipation of the mind" of reform and opening-up, the support of the central and local governments, and favorable geographic and environmental conditions—have combined to make Shenzhen a symbol of China's special economic zones.

9. The "Contract Responsibility System": The Pioneer of China's Reform

Located in the east of Fengyang County, Anhui Province, lies a village named Xiaogang. For decades following the founding of the People's Republic of China in 1949, Xiaogang was unable to extricate itself from poverty, and became known as the county's "village of three dependences" (i.e., dependence on buy-backs for food, dependence on government relief for money, and dependence on loans for production). By the end of 1977, Xiaogang commune members had nothing left, and almost every villager—whether young or old, man or woman—had begged for food at one time or another. Then, in December 1978, 18 Xiaogang farmers risked their lives to sign a secret agreement. The result was the birth of the "contract responsibility system" (also known as the "household responsibility system) and the launch of China's rural reform. In this way, the poor and remote village of Xiaogang became the pioneer of China's economic reform.

Under the contract responsibility system, rights to land use and other means of production, as well as production tasks, are contracted out from the agricultural collective to individual farmer households. This system, while maintaining the unified management required by China's collective agricultural economy, involves the transfer of land use rights to individual farmers by means of long-term contracts. In accordance with the rights stipulated in the contract, the contracting household can make independent operating decisions (such as with respect to planting or cultivation); and, after meeting state and collective quotas, can sell any surplus crops on the open market. The contract responsibility system is the great creation of Chinese farmers who were compelled to take risks in order to survive, and the fruit of China's rural economic reform.

As a bottom-up reform effort, the contract responsibility system can be traced back to the early 1960s. At that time, Liu Shaoqi and Deng Xiaoping presided over China's central economic work and advocated a program called "three freedoms and one guarantee" (freedom to cultivate private plots, sell surpluses on free markets, and engage in sideline occupations with full responsibility for profits and losses; and a fixed output quota for which each household

would bear responsibility). In 1977, after Deng reassumed power, his right-hand man Wan Li was appointed as CPC first secretary of Anhui Province. During his inspection visit to Anhui, Wan once asked a farmer whether he had any requests. The farmer replied: "I want to have enough to eat." Wan then asked if the farmer had any other requests, to which the farmer answered: "Can I exchange my dried sweet potatoes for grain?" Overcome with emotion, Wan issued a circular letter in Anhui Province calling for the autonomy of production teams, consideration of farmers' interests in the process of grain distribution, authorization and encouragement of commune members' legitimate sideline occupations, and the return of expropriated private plots to commune members.

Taking notice of Wan Li's letter, the *People's Daily* published an article on March 27, 1978, entitled "Resolutely Implement the Policy of Distribution According to Work." Although the article sparked major controversy at the time, Anhui's contract responsibility system was nevertheless implemented—albeit in secret. Wan offered his words of encouragement to Chen Tingyuan, CPC secretary of Fengyang County: "It's okay to go it alone."

In 1980, Wan Li became minister of the State Agricultural Commission. Under his guidance, the contract responsibility system was vigorously promoted, setting in motion a wave of economic reform. By 1983, 99 percent of production brigades in rural China

had implemented the contract responsibility system. China's agriculture, too, achieved rapid growth. From 1977 to 1984, grain output soared from 280 million tons to 410 million tons (an average growth rate of 5.35 percent per year), resolving China's long-term grain shortage problem. According to research done by the International Monetary Fund, about three-fourths of China's agricultural growth during this period is attributable to the implementation of the contract responsibility system, while the remainder was the result of rising agricultural commodity prices. After 1985, China experienced slowing growth in grain output. This slowdown, however, did not mean that the stimulative effect of the contract responsibility system had worn off, but rather resulted from the fact that growth in grain demand had entered a period of stability.

The achievements of the contract responsibility system are not limited to its solving of China's hunger problem. In addition to enabling farmers to gain operational autonomy over their land, the system also liberated China's agricultural labor force by allowing farmers the freedom to choose their own occupations. Hundreds of millions of rural surplus laborers migrated eastwards and took part in an economic miracle—the development of China's eastern coastal region. Meanwhile, China's burgeoning township-and-village enterprises, set up by farmers who opted to "leave the soil but not the countryside," also emerged as a new and powerful force—and a serendipitous byproduct of the contract responsibility system.

All of these achievements served to significantly expedite China's economic development and urbanization processes. The rural population as a percentage of the total population fell from 82 percent in 1978 to 55.1 percent in 2007, while agricultural labor as a percentage of the total labor force dropped from 70.5 percent to 41.7 percent over the same period.

With the deepening of China's reform efforts, however, the contract responsibility system also needs to be intensified. In essence, the system not only marked the beginning, but could spell the end, of Chinese rural reform. Since entering the 21st century, China has met with agricultural inefficiency, land abandonment, and the steady fall of agricultural commodity prices; all of these problems are linked to the limitations of the contract responsibility system. The system's initial aim was to resolve the food shortage and to boost the market supply of grain and oil; farmers were merely granted land use rights, while land ownership remained with the state. Even though the original contract clearly stated that the system would not be altered within a term of 30 or 50 years, frequent changes and adjustments have indeed been made. Under these conditions of operational uncertainty, farmers have increasingly lacked the confidence to devote efforts simultaneously to raising crops in the short term while maintaining the land's long-term fertility.

Unless reforms of the contract responsibility system are continued in the direction of enhanced property rights, the further progress of China's economic reform will be impeded. Indeed, the fact that, after 30 years of reform, the "three-dimensional rural problem" (agriculture, farmers, and rural areas) was again addressed in the CPC's "Central Document No. 1" indicates that the continued amelioration of the contract responsibility system has become a matter of great urgency. To this end, the reform of forest property rights—the promotion of which has already begun on a large scale—represents a positive step in the right direction.

10. The Bashan Steamer Conference

On the afternoon of September 2, 1985, the Yangtze River cruise ship *Bashan* left the shores of Chongqing and slowly set sail for Wuhan. At the time, the newly-operational *Bashan* Steamer was China's most luxurious cruise ship. That afternoon, the ship welcomed as its guests a distinguished group of economists, numbering in the dozens, from both China and abroad. Together, they discussed and debated the country's economic strategies, policies and direction, in what would later be called "a brainstorming [session] at China's turning point."

Foreign scholars in attendance included James Tobin (American economist, Yale University professor, and Nobel laureate); János Kornai (Hungarian economist and leading researcher in the field of transition economics); Sir Alexander Cairncross (chancellor of the University of Glasgow and former head of Britain's Govern-

ment Economic Service); Adrian Wood (former chief economist at the UK's Department for International Development); Aleksandar Bajt (leading economist of the former Yugoslavia); Wlodzimierz Brus (professor at the University of Oxford); Otmar Emminger (former president of Deutsche Bundesbank); Michel Albert (honorary chairman of the French insurance company AGF and director of Crédit Lyonnais); Minoru Kobayashi (chairman of the Industrial Bank of Japan); and Edwin Lim (then director of the World Bank's representative office in China).

In addition to the foreign experts, the *Bashan* Steamer's guests also included over a dozen Chinese scholars considered to be China's "third generation of economists." Among them, those 60 years of age or older included Xue Muqiao (then advisor to the State Commission for Economic Restructuring ["SCER"]); An Zhiwen (deputy director of the SCER and a member of the Central Advisory Commission); Tong Dalin (deputy director of the SCER); Ma Hong (deputy secretary-general of the State Council and director of the Development Research Center of the State Council ["DRC"]); and Liu Guoguang (vice-president of the Chinese Academy of Social Sciences ["CASS"]). Those between 50 and 59 years of age included Dai Yuanchen (research fellow at the CASS Institute of Economics); Yang Qixian (deputy director of the SCER); Zhou Shulian (deputy director of the CASS Institute of Industrial Economics); Gao Shangquan (deputy director of the SCER); Wu Jinglian (senior research fellow at the DRC); Zhao

Renwei (deputy director of the CASS Institute of Economics); Zhang Zhuoyuan (director of the CASS Institute of Finance and Trade Economics); and Chen Jiyuan (member of the CASS Institute of Rural Development). Finally, domestic scholars below the age of 50 included Xiang Huaicheng (deputy director of the Comprehensive Planning Department of the Ministry of Finance); Hong Hu (secretary-general of the SCER); Lou Jiwei (deputy head of the financial and banking office group of the General Office of the State Council); Li Kemu and Tian Yuan (both members of the DRC); and Guo Shuqing (doctoral research fellow at the CASS).

As the whistle sounded and the *Bashan* Steamer proceeded along its easterly course, passengers were treated to the spectacular sights of the ancient village of Baidi, the Three Gorges, and the Daning and Xiaoning rivers. The purpose of this voyage, however, was not to enjoy the beautiful scenery, but to hold a meeting—China's "International Seminar on Macroeconomic Management," jointly convened by the State Commission for Economic Restructuring, the Chinese Academy of Social Sciences and the World Bank. With all outside disturbances left behind on the mainland, the steamer set out from Chongqing along the Yangtze River and, only five days later, arrived at its destination of Wuhan. Yet the influence on the Chinese economy of this short week-long cruise—later dubbed the "*Bashan* Steamer Conference"—would extend for more than 20 years after it touched shore, and can still be felt even today.

After 1979, not long after China's reform and opening-up drive was launched, the economy experienced rapid growth. By the fourth quarter of 1984, however, bank credit growth was out of control, investment had soared, and prices were rising by as much as 10 percent annually. Excessive demand, an overheating economy, rising inflation and a foreign trade deficit posed daunting challenges to Chinese policymakers. In particular, China's first bout of inflation since the launch of reforms caused a state of frenzied buying to erupt. Chinese citizens began to buy up almost everything in sight (whether they had a use for it or not), from big-ticket items like televisions to smaller things like matches and cigarettes.

At that time, the reality was that China had been unable to replicate the success of rural reform in China's cities. Even though the *Resolution of the CPC Central Committee on Reform of the Eco-*

nomic System had already been enacted (in October 1984) and the development of the "socialist commodity economy" had been determined as the direction of China's reform, key questions still remained unanswered. What was the aim of reform? How exactly should a "planned commodity economy" be run? How should the relationship between the government and state-owned enterprises (SOEs) be managed with respect to urban reform? How should China cope with overheated investment and inflation of the renminbi? At the time, China's policymakers and economists were still seeking the answers to these most fundamental questions.

It was precisely the goal and agenda of the *Bashan* Steamer Conference to tackle these tough questions and issues. The conference, however, was not so much a discussion forum as an opportunity for the driving forces of China's reform to consult with Western economists and the pioneers of Eastern Europe's economic transition.

These foreign guests—who had a wealth of personal experience with the Western economic system—repeatedly stressed that China's economic reforms should draw valuable lessons from the modernization processes of Western nations. In particular, they pointed out that, in regard to achieving macroeconomic balance and social equity while simultaneously maintaining the vitality of free competition at a microeconomic level, China's conditions would enable it to outperform Western countries.

With respect to which model should be adopted for China's economic reforms, for example, János Kornai proposed market coordination with "macroeconomic regulation and control." Wlodzimierz Brus

believed that the ownership system should be diversified; and that the state should maintain strong control over the investment process to ensure the future structure of productive forces, control the distribution of income to achieve rational job placement and abundant employment opportunities, and control foreign economic relations to make sure that economic changes abroad do not cause large fluctuations in China's domestic economy. The viewpoint of Leroy Jones, the youngest foreign participant at the *Bashan* Steamer Conference, was even more original. Jones noted that, even though Chinese reform theory called for the establishment of a complete market system, China was still a developing country; as such, he noted, direct control of capital and foreign exchange was still necessary for China, and capital and foreign exchange markets should not be fully opened until much later.

In regard to the relationship between the market and the government, Alexander Cairncross, the former head of Britain's Government Economic Service, adhered to his opinion. After the Second World War, Cairncross noted, Britain underwent a gradual shift from a controlled economy to a market economy. First, the British government abandoned commodity price control and goods and materials distribution; then, it gave up the job allocation system; and, lastly, foreign-exchange control was given up. Moreover, Cairncross pointed out, giving up administrative control does not mean that the state abandons economic intervention. James Tobin and Wlodzimierz Brus, in their addresses, also affirmed the significance of these foreign experiences vis-à-vis China's reforms. They emphasized the importance of maintaining economic stability during the reform process and indicated that, while economic means are not yet mature, China should not hesitate to adopt administrative measures. Tobin and Brus also added the caveat, however, that it is easy for provisional administrative control measures to become permanent measures and that it is imperative to prevent this from occurring.

Finally, János Kornai offered his advice. Reform, he noted, would not be a smooth process; setbacks and even reversals of previous gains would be likely to occur. He suggested two reasons for this. First, the economic system is rather complex; once a large mistake is made during the course of reform, economic turbulence would ensue. The best way to resolve such a scenario would be to use administrative measures. Second, short-term difficulties would be practically inevitable. In the event of such difficulties, temporary administrative control measures should be adopted to stabilize the economy, but long-term goals must not be abandoned in the process. Third, China's huge administrative body would be difficult to reform due to the power and authority that it wields. Revoking the authority of an administrative agency, Kornai noted, would require overcoming difficulties, avoiding setbacks and, most importantly, the determination and will of China's leadership.

In a sense, it was the frankness of the guests and the open-mindedness of the hosts at this conference over two decades ago that helped push China's reform theory and ideology to new heights of understanding and awareness. In 2005, 20 years after this historic cruise, the Chinese economic journal *Comparative Studies* published a review essay called *Famous International Scholars and Experts on Chinese Economic Reform*, written shortly after the conference by its youngest participant, Guo Shuqing, who was only 29 years old at the time. Today, Guo is the chairman of China Construction Bank Corporation. Given the progress to date of China's reform initiative, it is evident that Chinese economists and top-level policymakers not only gained valuable knowledge and experience from the *Bashan* cruise that are still relevant today, but have also demonstrated persistence and innovation in carrying out the work of economic reforms. In this sense, China proved itself to be a "good student"—which is the reason that the *Bashan* Steamer Conference has become endowed with such significance.

11. The "Double-Track Pricing System": from Planning to Market

The first difficulty encountered during China's economic reform was the "pricing problem."

Under China's planned economy, the prices of practically all commodities were set by the state. A box of matches might have cost 0.02 yuan, for example, while 500 grams of salt may have sold for 0.13 yuan. This situation lasted for 28 years. In particular, after economic reforms were introduced into China's cities, market competition would be impossible to achieve without free pricing. The resulting "pricing dilemma" became a formidable and seemingly insurmountable obstacle along China's path to economic reform.

The most prominent situation in which this was demonstrated

was that, since the prices of primary industry products (such as energy and raw materials) were too low and the prices of processing industry products too high, the primary industry was increasingly unable to keep up with the development of the processing industry. The State Council, after convening several meetings to discuss the issue of price reform, found that minor adjustments would be unable to solve any problems and that major adjustments could not be sustained by the economy.

Xu Jing'an, who worked for the State Commission for Economic Restructuring at the time, later recalled: "If the price of coal were slightly increased, electricity and rail transport prices would go up and business costs would rise. But sales prices couldn't be altered, so what could we do? Later, we figured out a solution: After adjusting the price of coal, anyone who gained profits would have them reclaimed by the state, while anyone who suffered losses would be compensated. What was the end result? For those who profited, the state did not reclaim their profits; and for those who suffered losses, the state had to subsidize them. No matter how many plans were made, not a single one of them worked."

To address this problem, the young scholar Tian Yuan and others at the State Council's Price Research Center suggested making large-step adjustments to the severely distorted pricing system. In

contrast, Zhou Xiaochuan, Lou Jiwei, Li Jiange and others proposed the use of quick, small-step adjustments to continually regulate the price system and progressively close in on the market equilibrium price. Since even minor changes to the pricing system could affect the entire social interest structure or cause an unforeseeable chain reaction, China's policymakers, after weighing the ups and downs of various "solutions," had difficulty reaching any conclusions.

The breakthrough came in 1984 at Mogan Mountain (Moganshan), an offshoot of the Tianmu mountain range. This famous mountain, located in Deqing County, Zhejiang, is said to be the place where the famous swordsmith couple Gan Jiang and Mo Ye forged their swords. With beautiful scenery, cool temperatures and refreshing breezes, Mogan Mountain is renowned as the "Number One Mountain South of the Yangtze River." From September 3 to 10, 1984, the first National Symposium for Young Economic Scientists—which later became famous as the "Moganshan

Conference"—was held at this mountain.

Under the organization of Wang Qishan, Zhu Jiaming, Lu Mai, Zhou Qiren and Gao Liang, 124 young reformists—including both scholars and officials—gathered together at Moganshan, filled with a deep sense of responsibility. The conference was divided into seven working groups (such as pricing, rural areas and society), with participants comparing notes and exchanging views along the way. Through academic discussion and the drafting of policy recommendations, these ambitious reformists, for the first time, actively took part in the institutional reform of their country. In doing so, they recaptured the traditional sentiment of "carrying the burden of national salvation" that has been a part of Chinese history for thousands of years.

At this pioneering event in the history of Chinese economic reform ideology, the discussion that had the greatest impact on China's later reforms was the intense debate over pricing reforms. Initially, the debate was between the "price adjustment school" and the "price liberalization school." The price liberalization school, represented by Northwest University graduate student Zhang Weiying, advocated easing price controls in one step or multiple steps and implementing prices based on market supply and demand. The price adjustment school, in contrast, held that, under a predominantly planned economy, suddenly releasing price controls would be unrealistic. While the market was not yet mature, they contended, the market equilibrium price would be difficult to achieve; and, even if it were achieved, it might not be optimal.

As a result of having worked for the central government in close contact with the top tiers of leadership, Wang Qishan, Li Xianglu (secretary of the then CCCPC General Secretary Zhao Ziyang), Kong Dan (secretary of State Council member Zhang Jinfu), Xu Jing'an and others brought with them a great deal of knowledge

encompassing the overall situation, thereby enabling the conference to pay more attention to reality and actual practice. Stirred by the enthusiastic atmosphere that enveloped the conference, a group of scholars led by Hua Sheng, He Jiacheng, Jiang Yue, Gao Liang and Zhang Shaojie amalgamated the views of each side to form a middle-of-the-road approach: a double-track system of price reform that integrated price adjustment and price liberalization.

Finally, Xu Jing'an wrote this achievement into a report entitled *Two Approaches to Pricing Reform*, and submitted copies to central government officials. On September 20, 1984, State Council member Zhang Jinfu, head of the Planning Commission and of the Commission for Economic Restructuring, offered his praise: "The 'two approaches to pricing reform' advanced at the National Symposium for Young Economic Scientists is of excellent reference value." On October 10, Zhao Ziyang remarked: "The 'two approaches to pricing reform' really opens the mind. The overall theme is how to combine price liberalization with price adjustment, and apply them flexibly. By guiding the matter along its course of development, we can not only avoid a shock but also solve the problem at hand. Guangdong's approach of modifying its commodity price management system as a first step, the path taken by Jiangsu's township-and-village enterprises, the collaborative reduction of coal prices, and the price ratio that resulted from the state's

mass purchases of grain and cotton at an "excess purchase price" (above quota price) were all, in essence, successful examples of combining price liberalization and adjustment."

Characterized by the coexistence of planned and market prices (with the latter higher than the former), a gradual reduction in allocated proportions, and a progressive expansion in market share, the double-track system became the guiding philosophy of China's price reform. The double-track system of pricing transformed the large-scale system of price reform into several smaller and manipulable systems, effectively circumventing major risks. Of even greater significance is the fact that the double-track system not only partly rectified China's inequitable pricing system, but also broke through the highly rigid price management system, fueling reforms of the planning and goods and materials systems.

This was a major breakthrough for China's planned economy, which laid the foundation for the country's commodity economy system. Later, many of China's economic reforms adopted the "double-track system" approach. Furthermore, practically all later reforms—especially the initial phases of special economic zones and open coastal cities prior to the opening up of the Chinese mainland—began with experimental pilot sites before progressively expanding in scale and scope.

The clear advantage of the double-track system is that, by retaining the "old track," the continued progress of pricing reforms was facilitated. If price controls had been suddenly released, the economy would not have been able to bear it, and society would have been unable to accept the market-price concept all at once. Nevertheless, the double-track system also gave rise to certain difficulties and problems, including conflicts between the new and old system, systemic loopholes, and corruption spawned as a byproduct.

After numerous compromises, deadlocks and detours, the double-track pricing system finally made its successful leap from planning to market. In the end, the double-track system ideology defeated several seemingly promising choices and, in the process, became a symbol of China's progressive, dual-system approach to reform.

12. The Development of Pudong

In the earliest existing photograph of Pudong, dated to the late-19th century, Pudong's Lujiazui area was a completely empty space, with the exception of a single tree.

Located at the intersection of the Huangpu River and the estuary of the Yangtze River, Pudong has an area of 552 square kilometers, equivalent to about one-tenth the land area of Shanghai. In 1918, Sun Yat-sen sighed emotionally as he looked over this barren land, and remarked: "If Pudong were to develop to the level of Puxi [a section of Shanghai separated from Pudong by the Huangpu River], China would be extraordinary." Chen Yi, the first Mayor of Shanghai after the founding of the People's Republic of China, expressed a similar sentiment, describing Pudong as a "virgin land."

During the 1980s, after the launch of China's economic reform

and opening-up program, and while Jiang Zemin was serving as Mayor of Shanghai, the development of Pudong was placed on the agenda. In 1986, *Shanghai Overall Planning Scheme* was submitted to the State Council, which ultimately ratified it, thereby officially sanctioning the development of Pudong. In May 1988, Shanghai organized and convened the International Symposium on the Development of Pudong New Area, attended by over 100 domestic and foreign experts.

However, most crucial to the opening up of Shanghai and the development of the Pudong district were Deng Xiaoping's seven consecutive years of visits (1988 to 1994) to Shanghai during the Spring Festival, the speeches he gave there, and the hopes he left behind.

In January 1990, Deng Xiaoping—the chief architect of China's economic reform and opening-up policy—made a visit to Shanghai for the third consecutive year. By this time, Jiang Zemin had been transferred to the central government and Zhu Rongji was serving as the mayor and Party chief of Shanghai. On his previous two visits, Deng had simply taken a quiet stroll on the lakefront at Building No. 1 Xijiao Hotel and rarely voiced his views in public. This time, however, after carefully listening to the comments of

municipal Party committee members and veteran comrades, Deng for the first time advanced the idea of "developing and opening up Pudong." On March 3 of the same year, during talks with leading comrades of the Central Committee, Deng reiterated his thought with greater definitude: "Shanghai is our trump card. By developing Shanghai, we shall be taking a shortcut." On April 18, then PRC Premier Li Peng announced in Shanghai: "The CPC Central Committee and the State Council have decided to speed up the development of Shanghai's Pudong area by making Pudong an economic and technological development zone and implementing special economic zone policies."

Sha Lin, chief executive of the Pudong Development Office, received this information immediately. The next morning, he promptly set up two large signs, with white characters on a green background, at the exit of the Pudong tunnel. The signs read

"Pudong Development Office of the Shanghai Municipal People's Government" and "Planning and Design Research Institute of Pudong, Shanghai." On May 1, 1990, Shanghai's municipal government announced, both to China and to the world, 10 preferential policies for the opening up of Pudong New Area.

Deng Xiaoping's ideas continued to spring forth. On February 15, 1991, the first day of the Spring Festival, Party and government leaders gathered in Shanghai to exchange Lunar New Year greetings. As the gathering was about to conclude, Deng made an unexpected address to the leading cadres of Shanghai: "You must seize the remainder of the 20th century, and grasp its final opportunities to accelerate development."

Three days later, Deng Xiaoping arrived at Shanghai's tallest and only recently completed building, New Jinjiang Hotel. While meeting with Zhu Rongji in the hotel's 41st floor revolving restaurant and looking over some maps and models of Pudong New Area, Deng delivered another address: "Developing Pudong District will have a great impact not just on the district itself but on all of Shanghai, which in turn will serve as a base for the develop-

ment of the Yangtze delta and the whole Yangtze basin. We must lose no time in developing Pudong District and persevere until construction is complete."

Deng Xiaoping sighed with emotion as he continued: "We are late in developing Pudong—late by at least five years. Back in 1984 and 1985, I felt that Shanghai should be developed, but at the time the resolve was not there." Deng believed that, whereas the development of Guangdong was aimed at Hong Kong and the development of Xiamen Special Economic Zone in Fujian was aimed at Taiwan, the development of Shanghai could be aimed at the entire world.

These two speeches given by Deng Xiaoping during the 1991 Spring Festival on the subject of Shanghai's development not only inspired Shanghai's policymakers, but also further strengthened the resolve of the entire nation to persist in and intensify its reform and opening-up efforts. At the 14th National Congress of the CPC held in 1992, Jiang Zemin secured his post as General Secretary of the CCCPC. The Congress further established Shanghai's national strategic position, which it described as "one dragon head and three centers." This meant that, with the development and opening up of Pudong as the "dragon head," Shanghai would be built into an economic, financial and trade center ("three centers"), thereby spurring on "leapfrog" development in the Yangtze River economic belt.

Thereafter, Shanghai's position immediately surged from "rearguard" to "vanguard," not only ensuring its own steady development, but also spurring on double-digit annual economic growth in the peripheral regions of Kunshan and Suzhou, the entire Yangtze Delta, and even Anhui and Jiangxi provinces. The Yangtze Delta thus became the most active region of the economy during China's second phase of reform and opening-up.

Pudong New Area proved to be even more of a frontrunner than Shanghai. The first goal set forth for the development and opening-

up of Pudong was for the area's GDP to reach 50 billion yuan (over half of Shanghai's GDP at the time) by the turn of the century. In fact, Pudong's GDP in the year 2000 actually rose to 100 billion yuan. In 2007, the district's GDP climbed to 275 billion yuan. During the first 18 years since development began in 1990, Pudong enjoyed average annual economic growth of about 18 percent.

While Pudong's development led to institutional innovation, it also resulted in the emergence of certain gray areas that sowed the seeds of trouble for Shanghai's growth. The most unsettled debate over such a gray area concerns the practice of "wholesale land leasing" that emerged alongside the development of Pudong. Due to a shortage of funds, the Shanghai Finance Bureau (through the Pudong Development Office) employed a technique of "empty fiscal operations." The Finance Bureau issued checks to development companies, which, in turn, presented them to the Shanghai Land Administration Bureau in exchange for wholesale plots of land. The Land Administration Bureau, however, could not retain these payments, and had to remit them back to the Shanghai Bureau of Finance. This method enabled selected development companies in

the Pudong development zone to acquire vast amounts of land and capital. Subsequently, this strategy was mass-duplicated and applied to urban development and construction throughout Shanghai. Government officials and businessmen alike gradually looked on wholesale land leasing as a "nuclear reactor" for GDP growth and wealth accumulation; from 1988 to 2005, the Shanghai Municipal Government raised a total of about 2.73 trillion yuan from wholesale land leasing to use as investment capital for the development of Shanghai. Shanghai's real estate market, too, exploded into a state of frenzy. The proportion of municipal GDP held by the realty industry rose from 0.5 percent in 1990 to 7.3 percent in 2005, making real estate Shanghai's third largest industry following the information and commercial logistics industries.

On September 24, 2006, the 15th Secretary of the Shanghai CPC Municipal Committee, Chen Liangyu, who pushed "wholesale land leasing" and "urban management" to the point of lunacy and corruption, was removed from office and investigated. The same year, the State Council approved the full-scale launch of the new "Pudong Integrated Support Reform Pilot Area."

13. The Scientific Outlook on Development

In 2003, the Chinese economy sustained its momentum of high growth that had already lasted for 25 years. A noteworthy statistic from that year is that, for the first time, China's GDP per capita exceeded US$1,000. The development paths of many countries indicate that, when per-capita GDP tops the US$1,000 mark, the country's economic and social development enters a critical period.

During the spring of 2003, however, the Chinese people's joy was met with the onslaught of the SARS epidemic. Although this public health crisis lasted less than three months and affected only a few provinces, it resulted in large economic losses, especially in the industries of tourism, commerce and services, aviation, transportation and construction, as well as certain manufacturing industries. As a result of the epidemic, China's second-quarter economic growth dropped to 6.2 percent, and normal economic,

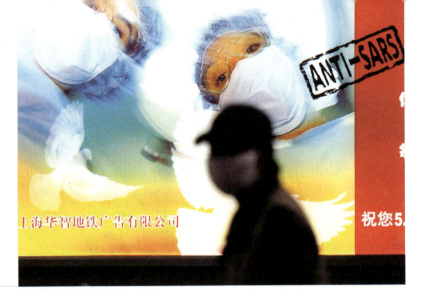

social and political life was disrupted.

It was precisely at this time that Li Junru, vice president of the CPC Central Committee's Party School, made an important realization. The occurrence of the SARS epidemic, and the painstaking efforts to combat it, led Li to the following insight: As China promoted economic growth and raised people's living standards, it would also have to do a good job in public health, education and other areas, and make caring for the people an important priority in the Party's work.

It was the Chinese government's caring and concern for its people, Li believes, that led to dramatic changes in the CPC's governing philosophy, namely, the Scientific Outlook on Development advanced at the Third Plenary Session of the 16th CCCPC in October, 2003. Li summarized the essence of this new philosophy as "striving to put people first; establishing a view of comprehensive, coordinated and sustainable development; promoting the all-around development of the economy, society and people; and persisting in the orchestrated planning of urban and rural development, regional development, socioeconomic development, the harmonious development of man and nature, and domestic development and opening-up."

In addition to stressing economic development, the Scientific

Outlook on Development, for the first time, emphasized the importance of social development.

Chinese president Hu Jintao first advanced the guiding ideology of the Scientific Outlook on Development during his inspection tour of Guangdong in April 2003. It was in June of the same year, at the national counter-SARS summary meeting, that he formally used the term "Scientific Outlook on Development" for the first time.

In his subsequent analysis, Li Junru pointed out that the battle against SARS was an important and direct factor in the formation of the Scientific Outlook on Development. However, Li further noted that, while the SARS epidemic was the immediate cause that spurred the genesis of the Scientific Outlook on Development, the underlying causes were resource and environmental problems brought by rapid economic growth, uneven development between urban and rural areas, and unbalanced regional development.

In 2003, China's GDP accounted for 4 percent of global GDP. In the same year, figures for the country's resource consumption as a percentage of world consumption were even more startling: 7.4 percent for petroleum, 31 percent for raw coal, 30 percent for iron ore, 21 percent for steel, 25 percent for aluminum oxide, and 40 percent for cement. The excessive development of high polluting and high energy-consumption industries had caused China's eco-

logical environment to incur heavy damage.

By 2003, a trend of rising raw materials prices had emerged worldwide. With respect to steel, for instance, China's industrial development model of large-scale raw materials imports and steel

product exports was unable to prevent or stabilize soaring iron ore prices worldwide. Massive demand caused a breakdown in the price equilibrium of world industrial raw materials. The negotiated price for iron ore began to climb in 2003 and, by 2005, had risen almost 70 percent, placing unprecedented cost pressure on the Chinese manufacturing industry. China's industrial production model was facing a challenge.

In response, at the 16th National Congress of the CPC, China advanced the goal of "building a well-off society in an all-around way". This plan would entail 20 years of efforts to build a "high-level" well-off society capable of sustaining a population of over one billion people. Although China, having undergone the preceding 20-plus years of reforms and development, could already be considered a well-off society, it remained a "low-level" one at best, marked by the existence of deficiencies and highly uneven development.

The same year that China introduced the Scientific Outlook on Development, a series of corresponding policy measures was also adopted. In early 2003, in response to the illegitimate practices of some employers and companies—including embezzlement, defaulting on wages of rural workers, and discriminatory practices concerning the employment of rural workers and the education of their children—the State Council issued a policy document calling

for the lawful rights and interests of rural workers to be guaranteed and upheld, and launched a large-scale initiative to help them recover wages in arrears.

In April 2003, following the Sun Zhigang Incident, the State Council specially convened an executive meeting, at which the decision was made to abolish the *Custody and Repatriation Act* and provide vagrants and beggars with assistance services.

In November 2003, the Central Economic Work Conference stressed the importance of working for the public and of assuming power for the people. Also emphasized was the importance of firmly establishing a "correct view of political achievement," deemed a necessary prerequisite to carrying out the Scientific Outlook on Development and achieving comprehensive, balanced and sustainable development. Hu Jintao remarked: "We should put people at the top of our priority list and take the comprehensive development of man as our objective. With the fundamental interests of the people as our starting point, we should seek and promote development, continually satisfy the ever-increasing material and cultural needs of the people, effectively safeguard their economic, political and cultural rights and interests, and enable the fruits of development to benefit the entire citizenry."

14. Deng Xiaoping's "Southern Tour"

In 1992, Deng Xiaoping was selected as "Man of the Year" by the British *Financial Times* newspaper. The reason that this important mouthpiece of mainstream Western society conferred such an honor on the then 88-year-old Deng—who held no official office at the time—is that he had enabled the world's most populous country to make remarkable economic achievements.

"In January [of 1992], Deng Xiaoping went on a personal inspection tour of South China's special economic zones (SEZs), initiating a new wave of free-market economic reform across the country," recalled the *Financial Times*. "Deng praised the success attained by the SEZs and called for accelerated development. The result was the achievement of economic prosperity throughout the country. China's current rate of economic growth is almost

certainly at its highest ever."

The inspection tour mentioned above is a reference to Deng's 1992 "Southern Tour," the praises of which were sung in the patriotic Chinese song, *Story of Spring*.

In 1992, it had been two years since Deng Xiaoping retired. During those two years, China and the world had experienced a period of great turbulence. In which direction would the world develop? What would be the fate of socialism? What would China do in the future?

Faced with these momentous global issues, the Chinese people became divided over whether China should continue along the socialist road or turn onto the road of capitalism. The ensuing debate cast a long shadow on the future of China's reform and opening-up. At this moment of truth, Deng Xiaoping, the chief

architect of China's economic reforms, once again boldly stepped forward—after more than two years of silent contemplation.

From January 18 to February 21, 1992, the 88-year-old Deng Xiaoping, then an "ordinary Party member," made inspection visits to Wuchang, Shenzhen, Zhuhai and Shanghai. During his tour, he gave a systematic exposition of reform and opening-up at both theoretical and policy levels. While visiting the special economic zones of Shenzhen and Zhuhai, the habitually taciturn Deng talked almost incessantly. One time, on a ferry ride from Shenzhen to Zhuhai, Deng was so excited that he spoke non-stop for the entire one-hour duration of the ride.

According to official documents, Deng Xiaoping visited Shenzhen World Trade Center on January 20, 1992, and ascended to the 53rd floor. Looking down over the city, he commented: "We must achieve a well-off society by the end of the century and, after taking this step, catch up to the level of moderately developed countries. Only then will we have hope. Our time is limited!"

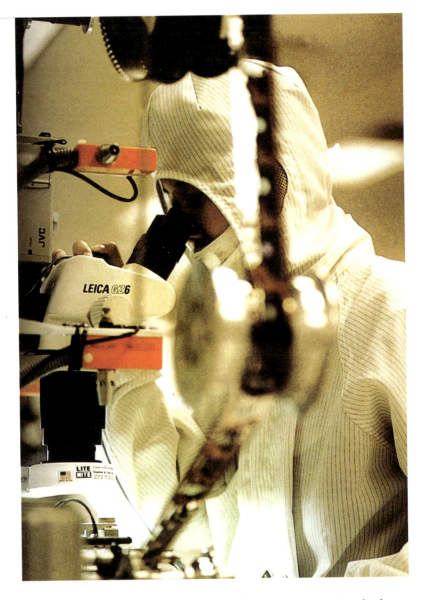

During this month-long Southern Tour—a journey in which every second was precious—Deng proposed many ideas that came to have a profound and far-reaching impact on the future of China's reforms.

In one speech, Deng remarked: "We should be bolder than before in conducting reform and opening to the outside, and have the courage to experiment. We must not act like women with bound feet. Once we are sure that something should be done, we should dare to experiment and break a new path. An important experience of Shenzhen is the courage to make breakthroughs. If we don't have the pioneering spirit, if we're afraid to take risks, if we have no energy and drive, we cannot break a new path, a good path, or accomplish anything new."

Deng added: "The reason some people hesitate to carry out the reform and opening-up policy and dare not break new ground is, in essence, that they're afraid it would mean introducing too many elements of capitalism and, indeed, taking the capitalist road. The crux of the matter is whether the road is capitalist or socialist. The chief criteria for making that judgment should be whether it promotes the growth of the productive forces in a socialist society, whether it increases the overall strength of the socialist state, and whether it raises people's living standards."

Deng also spoke of his interpretation of socialism, stating: "Whether there should be more planning or more market factors—this is not the fundamental difference between socialism and capitalism. A planned economy is not equivalent to socialism because there is planning under capitalism, too; and a market economy is not equivalent to capitalism because there are markets under socialism, too. Planning and market forces are both methods of controlling economic activity. The essence of socialism is

the liberation and development of the productive forces, the elimination of exploitation and polarization, and the ultimate achievement of prosperity for all."

Deng Xiaoping's Southern Tour speeches (including those excerpted above) became the final chapter of the *Selected Works of Deng Xiaoping*, acclaimed by Party history experts as the most definitive outline and summary of Deng Xiaoping Theory. On February 28, 1992, the CCCPC issued "Central Document No. 2 (1992)," a compilation of key statements made by Deng during his Southern Tour, and requested that copies be released expeditiously to all Party and government officials for study and implementation. In October that year, Jiang Zemin delivered his report to the 14th National Congress of the CPC, in which his nine-point summary of the "theory of building socialism with Chinese characteristics" was based largely on Deng's Southern Tour speeches.

Five years later, at the 15th National Congress of the CPC, Deng Xiaoping Theory was incorporated into the Party Constitution and established as the Party's guiding ideology alongside Marxism-Leninism and Mao Zedong Thought; by this time, the momentum of China's reform and opening-up drive had become irreversible. In 1999, Deng Xiaoping Theory was written into China's State Constitution.

Through his "distinctively Chinese" Southern Tour and the important speeches he made along the way, Deng Xiaoping laid down a cornerstone for the new millennium, and for the sound development of China into the 21st century and beyond.

During his Southern Tour, Deng made the important assertion that "science and technology is the first productive force."

This statement not only served to spur growth of China's knowledge-based economy during the mid- to late-1990s and enable scholars and experts to become high income-earners, but also removed the long-standing discrimination against China's intellectual class. The government also declared that all Chinese students studying abroad could return to their homeland; as a result, many of them indeed came back, often to pursue entrepreneurial opportunities. As more and more Chinese students returned home from their overseas studies, a growing class of intellectual elite emerged in China.

Ding Lei, who founded NetEase (the company that operates 163.com) and was ranked first in Forbes' 2003 list of China's richest people, once said during an interview: "One of the important reasons that I gave up my graduate studies after being accepted was that, at the time, against the backdrop of Deng Xiaoping's Southern Tour, I felt there were many opportunities—and that it would be better for me to step out into society on my own."

15. The Socialist Market Economy: China's New Reform Target

In 1989, China's GDP grew by 3.9 percent; and, in 1990 and 1991, the GDP growth rate was 5 percent and 7 percent respectively. These three years (1989 to 1991), it can be said, were the most difficult of China's 30 years of reform and opening-up to date. In December 1992, a full-page article in the state-owned *People's Daily* made the following seething attack: "A market economy would mean the abolishment of public ownership, that is to say, the negation of the Communist Party's leadership, the negation of our socialist system, and the introduction of capitalism."

On April 25, 1992, the usually calm and staid Tian Jiyun, vice premier of the State Council, used an unusually incisive tone in a speech delivered to the Central Party School: "The underlying is-

sue is to push the economy forward. We must not regard the fall of the Soviet Union as merely the result of one or two persons' mistakes. Such reasons are obviously important, but the underlying cause is that the mode of socialism adopted by the Soviet Union failed to attain a higher level of productivity development than capitalism, failed to bring the people happiness, and lost the support of the broad masses of the people."

On May 20, shortly after returning home from his Southern Tour, Deng Xiaoping visited Shougang Group (also known as Capital Iron and Steel Group) in western Beijing. Ignoring the beautiful factory area as he walked through it, Deng remarked: "When I speak, some people prevaricate, some people delay, and others actually get things done." He pointed out that engaging in reform is "like rowing upstream; not to advance is to drop back." He also made the following criticism: "There are some comrades among us who are content with [annual GDP growth of] 6 percent. That would mean the second stage [of development] would need the first stage to fill the gap, and reaching the third stage would be even harder... If we always maintained a rate of 6 percent, that would mean standstill and even regression; it would mean a lack

of progress, and a lack of development."

By this time, after three years of making observations and assessing the overall situation, General Secretary Jiang Zemin could hesitate no longer. On June 9, 1992, he arrived at the Central Party School near Beijing's Summer Palace. Facing 1.2 billion of his fellow countrymen—including Deng Xiaoping, who had promoted him to China's top leadership position—Jiang stood up to announce his decision. He wanted to make it clear that he not only would catch up with the pace of China's "second generation" of leadership (1976 to 1992), but would proceed even faster:

"In the report to the Party's 14th National Congress, we must ultimately settle upon a relatively scientific formulation endorsed by the great majority of comrades. This will facilitate further unity in the understanding and actions of the entire Party and nation, and facilitate the expedited establishment of a new socialist system. I am inclined towards using the formulation 'socialist market economic system.'"

The news spread quickly. Those who still equated the market economy with "bourgeois liberalization" were disheartened at once, while Du Runsheng, Yu Guangyuan, Wu Jinglian, Dong Fureng and other scholars whose ideas had been suppressed for three years beamed with joy at the news. Of course, among the celebrators were private business owners who, until this point, had lived in constant fear of being arrested and hauled off to prison. There were even reports of a few private entrepreneurs from Taizhou, Zhejiang, who, after confirming the veracity of the news, exchanged hugs and cried together in joy and relief.

At the 14th National Congress of the CPC, convened from October 12 to 18, 1992, Jiang Zemin delivered a report entitled *Speed Up the Pace of Reform, Opening-Up and Modernization to Achieve a Greater Victory for Socialism with Chinese Characteristics*. The Congress affirmed the guiding role for the entire CPC of Deng Xiaoping's

theory of building socialism with Chinese characteristics, clarified the reform goal of establishing a socialist market economic system, and demanded that the entire CPC seize the opportunity to accelerate development and focus on pushing economic development forward.

According to the Chinese government's definition, a socialist market economy is "a market economy under socialist conditions." Therefore, it not only possesses the general characteristics and regulations of a market economy, but also embodies a basic socialist system. The socialist market economy, as a form of market economy, utilizes the market as its primary means of allocating resources and operates through market mechanisms, i.e., the law of value. In this regard, the socialist market economy is no different from the capitalist economic system. The key distinguishing features of China's socialist market economy, according to Chinese officials, are twofold: economically, it operates through the joint development of multiple economic sectors (including the private sector) with the public sector as its base; politically, the socialist market economy is a market economy led by the CPC, macro-controlled by the Chinese government, and whose fundamental principle is the goal of achieving common prosperity.

In fact, as early as October 1984, the *Resolution of the CPC Cen-*

tral Committee on Reform of the Economic System (passed at the Third Plenary Session of the 12th CCCPC) had already advanced the notion of the "socialist commodity economy," establishing China's socialist economy as a planned commodity economy with public ownership as its base. On October 23, 1985, while meeting with a delegation of foreign visitors, Deng Xiaoping stated: "There is no fundamental contradiction between socialism and a market economy. The problem is how to develop the social productive forces more effectively." During his Southern Tour in early 1992, Deng further elaborated: "The proportion of planning to market forces is not the fundamental difference between socialism and capitalism. A planned economy is not equivalent to socialism; there is planning under capitalism, too. A market economy is not equivalent to capitalism; there are markets under socialism, too. Planning and market forces are both means of governing economic activity."

However, as a result of ideological constraints, the term "market economy" remained taboo and was shunned by government policy for a full decade. According to economist Wu Jinglian, defining the market economy as the main target of China's reforms was not only an ideological breakthrough but also "an epoch-making achievement."

Another person intimately familiar with this issue is Long Yongtu, former chief negotiator for China's resumption of GATT contracting party status and accession to the WTO. In 1987, during talks with his counterparts, Long found himself caught up in a thorny discussion over the concept of the market economy. During the discussion, he referred to China alternately as either a "planned commodity economy" or "planned economy with market regulation," but was simply unable to bring himself to use the term "market economy." A decade later, in 1997, Long looked

back and remarked: "Everyone says that we've been negotiating [WTO accession] for 10 years. Actually, we used six years to solve just one big problem, namely, to acknowledge that China is running a market economy."

In his memoirs, Chen Jinhua, former chairman of the State Commission for Economic Restructuring, offered a classic appraisal of the 14th National Congress of the CPC and, more importantly, of the socialist market economic system itself: "The socialist market economy theory is an epoch-making theory. It not only saved our economic system, but saved our social system as well."

On October 19, 1992, the 14th National Congress of the CPC came to a close. Just as the delegates were preparing to leave, Deng Xiaoping walked out from the side entrance leading to the platform. Dressed in a gray suit, Deng stepped forward—followed by seven newly-elected Standing Committee members—and greeted the Congress delegates. In an instant, the over 2,000 delegates in attendance rose to their feet and gave Deng a long standing ovation. After exchanging a few words of greeting with the delegates, the 88-year-old Deng offered his praise and encouragement to Jiang Zemin: "This was a very good Congress. I hope everyone keeps up the good effort." He then turned, waved his hand goodbye, and made his exit with grace and style.

16. Property Law: Equal Protection for Public and Private Property

On March 16, 2007, at the Fifth Session of the 10th NPC, *Property Law of the People's Republic of China* (hereafter "Property Law") was passed with a vote of 2,799 delegates in favor, 52 opposed, and 37 abstaining. Xinhua News Agency reported: "China is sending a signal of further expansion in reform and opening-up.... The socialist market economy is being further perfected, and political civilization has taken an important step forward."

From inception to implementation, this law that civil law scholars have described as "extremely complex to legislate" consumed a total of 14 years and went through eight rounds of deliberation by the Ninth NPC Standing Committee and 10th NPC and its Stand-

ing Committee before finally being signed into law. In the process, it set a record for the highest number of reviews of any single law draft in China's legislative history, as well as records for the longest time required for legislation, the greatest number of participants, and the highest frequency of amendment.

Not before the emergence of *Property Law* had China ever met with a piece of legislation filled with so many twists and turns. This circuitous complexity was the result not only of the vital importance of the bill itself, but also of ongoing social and economic changes during China's period of transition. An important component of civil law, China's *Property Law* is a fundamental law that addresses the recognition, use and protection of property and affects every level of society—from the nation as a whole to the livelihood of its people. In a sense, the gestation and passage of *Property Law* is a symbol of China's path towards progress.

To some extent, *Property Law* has taken on the important task of remedying the inequality between public and private rights that existed in China for several decades. As a result of the important institutional and conceptual changes that the *Property Law* bill entailed, large disputes inevitably emerged during the legislative process. Over the course of eight rounds of deliberation, the greatest debate was tied to the issue of private property. Jiang Ping, leader of the *Property Law* drafting group and a tenured professor at the China University of Political Science and Law, described this bill as one that "concerned the vital interests of every social stratum."

On July 10, 2005, a draft of *Property Law* was published to so-

licit opinions and comments from the general public. The debate that ensued was heated and intense. In 42 days, the legislature received a total of 11,543 suggestion letters. Among them, an open letter written by Gong Xiantian, a professor of law at Peking University, triggered a large-scale debate. In his letter, Gong denounced the *Property Law* bill as unconstitutional; the legislation, he contended, ignored the Chinese constitutional principle that "socialist public property is sacred and inviolable" in a reckless attempt to supersede it with the principle that "private property is sacred and inviolable." Gong also made the criticism that *Property Law* would accelerate the progression of privatization and result in polarization.

While a few scholars of planned-economy ideology and people with vested interests became a force of resistance to the enactment of *Property Law*, the public's main concerns were over the legislative details that would affect their immediate interests. The legislation's treatment of housing property rights attracted the attention of residents. "Building distinction ownership" received the attention of urban property owners. The bill addressed a variety of issues, ranging from the automatic renewal of land use rights after 70 years, to the ownership rights of green fields, roads, parking garages and houses for realty management use within building zones. Debate over the draft shifted back and forth between purely legal issues and practical matters in urgent need of standardization.

As the focus of public opinion, the *Property Law* bill was put on the legislative fast track. The bill went through a total of five rounds of deliberation during the 18-month period from June 2005 to December 2006. By the end of the revision process, some concessions had been made; while the "pursuant to laws and regulations" clause was retained, most of the "points of contention" were directly removed from the bill. After undergoing several rounds of simplification, revision and review, the bill was finally adopted by the NPC on March 16, 2007.

Property Law stipulates: "The property rights of the state, collective, individual, and any other holder of such rights shall be protected by laws and shall not be infringed by any institute or individual." The passage of this law served to affirm the legislative spirit and concept of equal protection of all forms of property. This was the first time that personal property was treated as equal to state property under Chinese law. In 2004, the NPC amended

Article 13 of the *Constitution of the People's Republic of China*, stipulating that "the lawful private property of citizens shall not be violated." This marked the first time that the issue of private property protection was raised in the Constitution, endowing the new Article 13 with epoch-making significance, while *Property Law* is the specific legal embodiment of this constitutional article.

For China, a country still in transition towards adopting a market economic system, the shift from precedence for public rights to equal protection of public and private

property was of great significance. The starting point of China's economic reforms was a planned economy, under which the government decided all economic activities and private property rights were nonexistent. Although such rights gradually emerged alongside China's reform and opening-up campaign, no laws were in place to protect and enforce them. The conventional thinking of several decades that government power, by its very nature, is greater than individual rights also engendered a discriminative attitude towards private property rights among the Chinese people.

The market depends on well-defined private property rights. As the fourth-century B.C. philosopher Mencius wrote: "A person with fixed property is a person of good moral character." Over 2,000 years later, the great eighteenth-century economist Adam Smith emphasized the benefits of ownership rights to society: "[If] people lack a sense of security about their property rights" and "are unable to receive the support of law concerning the fidelity of contracts," then "commerce and manufacturing cannot achieve lasting prosperity."

From another point of view, the "equitableness" principle embodied in the equal protection of all forms of property is also beneficial to the protection of state-owned assets. In the past, when public and state property rights enjoyed special status, state-owned property rights were ill-defined, and looting and property loss were frequent occurrences. Under equal protection, however, market competition mechanisms could effectively form; managers who infringed upon the property rights of others would not only be punished by law, but would also be restrained by market competition.

With respect to specific real-life matters, such as the expropriation of farmland, the demolition and relocation of urban housing, unified real property registration and other issues that concern

people's immediate interests, *Property Law* also provided equally specific provisions.

Gary Becker, a Nobel Prize laureate in Economics and professor at the University of Chicago, notes that, with the overwhelming passage of *Property Law*, the legalization of private property, and the CPC's decision in 2002 to legitimize the Party membership of private entrepreneurs, China's private economy had basically received an official affirmation. The newly enacted *Property Law*, Becker believes, will play an important navigating role in the future development of China's economy and society, a role that represents progressive reform rather than radical revolution.

17. The Imposition of Individual Income Tax

With ever-diversifying interests and a widening economic divide between the rich and the poor, China's reform policymakers realized as early as the mid-1980s the need to adjust the excessive income gap between members of society. To this end, the report submitted to the 13th National Congress of the CPC (held from October 25 to November 1, 1987) categorically stated that "effective measures must be adopted to adjust excessive personal income."

On September 25, 1986, the State Council issued *Provisional Regulations on Individual Income Adjustment Tax*, which took effect on January 1, 1987. At the time, the imposition of individual income adjustment tax was mainly for purposes of social equity, while increasing state revenue was a secondary motive. However, while the new personal income tax levy system did lead to progressively increasing tax revenues, it did not achieve its intended function of social regulation.

China's modern-day individual income tax has its roots in the 1950 policy document *Implementation Guidelines for National Tax Administration*, which stipulated that taxes be levied on salaries and wages earned. This early policy, however, was never implemented. After 1980, as China gradually opened its doors to the rest of the world, more and more profit-seeking foreigners came to China, and were soon making money in a variety of ways. A

base for levying individual income tax had finally emerged.

In September 1980, the *Individual Income Tax Law of the People's Republic of China* was promulgated and put into force. This was the first individual income tax law enacted since the founding of New China, as well as one of the first pieces of tax law passed since the launch of China's reform and opening-up drive. Under this new law, personal income tax would be levied on individuals with monthly income in excess of 800 yuan—an astronomical sum, given that the monthly wages of most Chinese citizens at the time ranged from 30 to 50 yuan. In effect, "individual income tax" became a tax category for foreigners.

In the years that followed, however, the Chinese people enjoyed increasingly diverse income channels and rising incomes. In 1986, China began to impose income tax on urban and rural self-employed industrial and commercial households, and a highly-publicized tax evasion scandal in 1989, involving Shanghainese pop singer Mao Amin, further fueled the public's growing interest in the high-income segment of society. By the end of the 1980s, individual income tax was no longer aimed solely at foreigners, but included China's small private businesses and high earners as well.

In the wake of China's economic development, the deepening of reform and opening-up, and especially the official declaration made at the 14th National Congress of the CPC of the goal of establishing a socialist market economic system, several flaws in the existing tax system were exposed. These included non-uniform tax policies in different regions, excessive tax burdens, limited transparency, an overly narrow tax

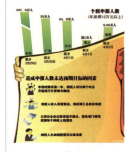

base, and poor tax collection methods. Finally, in 1993, China amalgamated the categories of "individual income tax," "individual income adjustment tax" and "income tax of urban and rural self-employed industrial and commercial households" into the single category of "individual income tax," with the new system becoming effective January 1, 1994.

Between 1987 and 2007, China's individual income tax revenues grew from 717 million yuan to 318.5 billion yuan, representing a gain of over 44,000 percent. The proportion of individual income tax revenues to total tax revenue also increased almost 20 times over the same period, from 0.34 percent to 6.4 percent. By 2007, individual income tax ranked as China's fourth largest source of tax revenue, surpassed only by value-added tax, enterprise income tax and business tax.

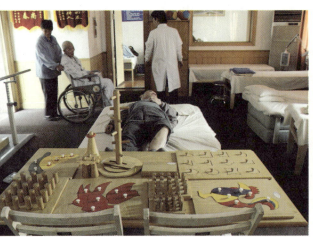

18. Split-share Structure Reform

During the first 14 years of the development of China's securities market, its greatest success was that of withstanding ideological attacks and ultimately gaining legal status. The price paid, however, was that, at the outset, the securities market faced questions and scrutiny over whether it represented socialist or capitalist ideology. In order for the securities market to survive, every effort had to be made to prove that it was indeed a socialist institution and that its function was to develop and expand the public sector. The result of this survival strategy was the emergence of the split-share structure system. Under this system, China's domestic A-shares were divided into "tradable shares" and "non-tradable

shares." Tradable shares refer to the publicly issued shares of a listed company that can be listed for trading on a stock exchange, while non-tradable shares are shares that have not been publicly issued and cannot be listed for trading. This split-share structure, whereby the shares of a single listed company are separated into tradable and non-tradable shares, is unique to the securities market of the Chinese mainland.

From the beginning, therefore, the Chinese securities market was built according to the design that would be most likely to gain acceptance, rather than that which would be most equitable. Attempting to "show its socialist stripes," the securities market became a channel for the allocation of state resources. In the meantime, individual and private enterprises, the driving force behind the market's operation, were excluded from the stock issuance market. In effect, China's stock markets served as a gigantic blood transfusion device for large- and medium-sized state-owned enterprises (SOEs). From issuing shares and bonds to asset restructuring, the goal was always the same—to revive SOEs deemed viable or important. During the first 13 years after the establishment of China's capital market, at least 95 percent of the funds raised in the stock market flowed into the coffers of SOEs.

The question of how to transform non-tradable shares into tradable shares and truly achieve "equal rights for equal shares" became the chief problem in the institutional reform of China's securities market.

The earliest attempt at such reform came in 2001, when Zhou Xiaochuan, then chairman of the China Securities Regulatory Commission (CSRC), and his colleagues advanced the notion

of reducing the holding of state-owned shares through their sale and circulation. In June of the same year, the State Council issued *Provisional Measures for Raising Social Security Funds through the Sale of State-owned Shares* (hereafter *Provisional Measures*), which prescribed that the reduction of state-owned stock be accomplished primarily through the issuance and sale of remaining state-owned shares. The provisional measures stipulated that all joint-stock companies (including foreign-listed companies) in which the state holds stock should sell state-owned shares equivalent to 10 percent of raised funds each time an initial public offering is made or additional shares are issued; and that all revenue derived from the sale of state-owned shareholdings be turned over to the National Social Security Fund.

As a result of serious discontent over the state-share reduction program, combined with the decision to lift restrictions on do-

mestic investors to purchase B-shares in February 2001 (criticized for causing Chinese domestic investors to rush into the B-share market as foreigners sold out, thus stranding domestic investors in a flat

market) and a lack of confidence in the supervisory institutions, the state-share reduction policy was heavily resisted by the market and finally terminated. On June 23, 2002, the State Council decided that the stipulation in *Provisional Measures* regarding the reduction of state-owned shareholdings via the securities market would no longer apply to domestic listed companies (although it still applied to enterprises listed overseas), and no replacement measures were introduced. The state-owned share reduction policy came to an official halt.

Half a year later, in December 2002, Shang Fulin, former president of the Agricultural Bank of China, was appointed chairman and Party chief of the CSRC. After joining the CSRC, the low-key and diplomatic Shang assigned himself an important task for his term in office: to vigorously promote reform of the split-share structure.

In early 2004, with share structure reform having lain quiet for nearly two years, Shang Fulin still faced resistance on multiple fronts. However, through long-term communication and cooperation, he was finally able to push through the legislation needed to achieve split-share structure reform. In early February of 2004, the State Council issued *Some Opinions of the State Council on Promoting the Reform, Opening and Steady Growth of Capital Markets* (commonly known as the "Nine Provisions of the State Council" and hereafter abbreviated as "Some Opinions"). This policy document stated the need to "actively and reliably resolve the split-share structure issue," adding that "the solution must respect market rules; contribute to the stability and development of the market; and genuinely protect the lawful rights and interests of investors, in particular public investors." The document also set out the aim of and the guiding principles for resolving the split-share structure issue.

After two years of extremely sluggish stock market performance, Shang Fulin, backed by the power and authority of the "Nine Provisions of the State Council," was able to advance his reform plan, stating: "The work [of share structure reform] is under control, and our thinking is aligned. We're ready to move forward." In accordance with the overall requirements of *Some Opinions* and guided by a coordinated, step-by-step approach, the CSRC went ahead with the reforms—starting on a trial basis.

On April 29, 2005, after obtaining the approval of the State Council, the CSRC issued *Circular on Issues concerning the Pilot Reform of the Split-share Structure of Listed Companies*, marking the official launch of pilot split-share structure reform. In September of the same year, share structure reform formally moved into the implementation phase. By June 2008, all of the more than 1,000 com-

panies listed in Shanghai or Shenzhen had completed their share reform. The Chinese stock market had entered a new stage of development.

All the while, the phraseology used to describe China's share structure reform was evolving—from "reduction of state-owned shares" to "full circulation," and finally "resolution of the split-share structure issue." In fact,

each of these terms contains different connotations. The phrase "reduction of state-owned shares" encompasses the concepts of stock market liquidity and the withdrawal of state-owned capital. "Full circulation" embodies the concept of the circulation and liquidation of non-tradable shares. Finally, the phrasing "resolution of the split-share structure issue" represents a reform concept, the essence of which is to transform non-tradable shares into tradable shares in order to achieve "equal rights for equal shares"; this is an important aspect of China's efforts to build an effective capital market system.

Split-share structure reform has enabled China's capital market to achieve major results (or, at the very least, to make preliminary progress) in several respects, such as enhancing the quality of listed companies; ensuring comprehensive governance of securities companies; developing strong institutional investors; and strengthening and perfecting the market legal system. With the interim success achieved from June 2001 to June 2008, the lingering ailment that had beleaguered China's securities market for over 10 years was finally eliminated, enabling the Chinese securities market to turn a new page.

19. Building a Well-off Society in an All-around Way

As early as 3,000 years ago, the term *xiaokang* appeared in the *Classic of Poetry*, the earliest collection of Chinese poems: *Min yi lao zhi, qi ke xiao-kang* ("The people indeed are heavily burdened, but perhaps a little ease may be got for them."). This is the first recorded usage of the term *xiaokang* in the history of Chinese civilization.

Around the first century BC, the *Conveyance of Rites* chapter of the Western-Han *Classic of Rites* gave a systematic exposition of the social model known as *xiaokang*, a term that has since become synonymous with "ideal society" in the Chinese language. Over two thousand years later, in 2002, the concept of *xiaokang* was

raised again—this time, in the political report to the 16th National Congress of the CPC. In this case, however, the mention of *xiaokang* was made as a declaration to China's 1.3 billion citizens. The attainment of the ideal of China's ancestors, the report stated, was only 20 years away from the Chinese masses of today; by seizing the development opportunities of the first two decades of the 21st century, China can be transformed into a *xiaokang* (or "well-off") society.

In October 2000, the strategic concept of "building a well-off society in an all-around way" was declared at the Fifth Plenary Session of the 15th CCCPC: "With the arrival of the new century, China has entered a new development stage of building a well-off society in an all-around way and accelerating the drive towards modernization."

On May 31, 2002, Jiang Zemin, then General Secretary of the CCCPC, reiterated in his speech to the Central Party School: "As we enter a new century, China has embarked on a new developmental stage, the stage of starting the full-scale construction of a

well-off society and accelerating socialist modernization." In the same year, the catchphrase "building a well-off society in an all-around way" was conceived at the 16th National Congress of the CPC.

The notion of an "all-around well-off society" is a quintessentially Chinese concept. It is a term rooted in history, but endowed with modern meaning, ranging from the age-old problem of ensuring adequate food and clothing for the people to the present-day task of modernization.

During the early stages of China's reform and opening-up, Deng Xiaoping referred to the goal of quadrupling China's gross national product (GNP) and achieving a well-off society as China's "lofty ambition." It was Deng who conceived the famous three-phase modernization strategy. The first phase (1981 to 1990)

consisted of doubling GNP and ensuring ample food and clothing for the Chinese people. The second phase (1991 to 2000) consisted of again doubling China's GNP and achieving a well-off society. Finally, the third and still ongoing phase (2001 to 2050) consists of quadrupling GNP and attaining the socioeconomic level of moderately developed countries.

As early as 1978, Deng Xiaoping began to expound his ideas for China's modernization target. In December of that year, at the Third Plenum of the 11th CCCPC, Deng announced the launch of the "Four Modernizations" (i.e., modernization of agriculture, industry, technology and defense). It was the following year, in December 1979, that Deng, at a meeting with Japanese Prime Minister Masayoshi Ohira, spoke for the first time of the notion of a *xiaokang* society. At that meeting, he described the rough target of the Four Modernizations as achieving an average per-capita GNP equal to that of moderately developed countries and realizing a society in which people lead relatively affluent lives, i.e., a *xiaokang* society.

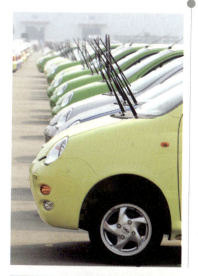

In 1982, the 12th National Congress of the CPC affirmed the *xiaokang* target advanced by Deng Xiaoping. This was the first time that the Party's National Congress adopted the concept of *xiaokang* and even made it the main goal for, and a preliminary symbol of, China's national economy and societal development. In spring of the following year, Deng visited China's

Jiangnan region. While taking a cruise on Lake Tai, he set out his views on how to build a *xiaokang* society. In 1984, he further clarified his vision: "[The goal of] *xiaokang* is to achieve per-capita GNP of US$800 by the end of the century."

What would China do after it had achieved a *xiaokang* society? Deng Xiaoping thought ahead to the 21st century. He stated that, although he would not live to see the new millennium, it was still his responsibility to set forth a goal beyond the year 2000. Once again, the first person to hear of Deng's goal was a foreigner. On April 30, 1987, at a meeting with Spanish vice prime minister Alfonso Guerra, Deng said: "When we have quadrupled [the size of China's economy] and reached the level of *xiaokang*—that can be called moderate change. By the middle of the 21st century, when we have approached the level of the world's developed countries—only that could be considered great change. By that time, the strength of socialist China and its role [in the world] will be different. We shall be able to make greater contributions to mankind."

In October 1987, the 13th National Congress of the CPC listed "the realization of a well-off society" as the qualitative target

of the second step of China's three-step development strategy. The Congress declared that China's modernization drive would achieve new and great progress, enabling the common people to lead relatively well-off lives, enjoy adequate food and clothing, and live and work in peace and contentment.

According to the three-step development strategy, China completed the first step (the doubling of 1980 GNP by 1990) in 1987, three years ahead of schedule; and the second step (the quadrupling of 1980 GNP by 2000) in 1995, five years ahead of schedule. The goal of quadrupling 1980 GNP per capita was also completed in 1997, three years ahead of schedule. By 2000, China had thus victoriously completed the first and second steps of the three-step development strategy and, on the whole, people throughout the country had attained a well-off standard of living. This was the fruitful achievement of China's reform, opening-up and modernization, and a milestone in the development history of the Chinese nation.

In October 2000, the Fifth Plenary Session of the 15th CCCPC stated that, from the dawn of the 21st century, China had embarked on a new stage of development—the stage of launching the full-scale construction of a well-off society and accelerating socialist modernization. The report submitted to the 16th National Congress of the CPC in November 2002 declared: "During the first 20

years of this century, we must concentrate on building a comprehensively well-off society of a higher standard to the benefit of over one billion people, further develop the economy, improve our democracy, advance science and education, stimulate culture, foster social harmony, and enrich the lives of our people."

20. The Birth of China's Stock Market

The Shanghai Stock Exchange (SSE) was founded under the direct leadership of then Mayor of Shanghai Zhu Rongji. On December 19, 1990, the SSE officially opened. Wei Wenyuan, the inaugural president of the SSE, recalls: "The SSE had only 30 listed stocks and 45,000 registered investors. When the exchange first opened, daily stock price movement was restricted to only 5 percent in either direction in order to prevent and control market fluctuations." On this day, however, it is said that Wei, after ring-

ing the opening bell, was so excited that he nearly collapsed on the floor. It was in this dramatic context that China's capital market finally came into being.

In fact, over 1,000 kilometers away from Shanghai, the opening bell of the Shenzhen Stock Exchange (SZSE) had already sounded 18 days prior to the SSE. Unlike the SSE, however, the SZSE had not yet received the formal approval of the State Council. Li Hao, Secretary of the CPC Shenzhen Municipal Committee, who had ordered that trading begin despite the absence of government approval, had no choice but to make a trip to Beijing to meet with authorities. At this critical moment, Zhou Jiannan, the father of current governor of the People's Bank of China (PBC) Zhou Xiaochuan, provided valuable assistance. CCCPC General Secretary Jiang Zemin asked Zhou Jiannan (who was also a minister of the former First Machine-building Industry and Jiang's former boss) to go on an inspection tour of Shenzhen. In the end, Zhou recommended that the SZSE indeed be established.

On July 3, 1991, the SZSE finally received the central government's go-ahead and had its status upgraded from "open on a trial basis" to "officially operational." By then, however, the Shenzhen bourse had already forfeited the honor of being China's first official stock exchange to the SSE—thus becoming "the early bird that *didn't* catch the worm." (Even years later, the SZSE has been unable to catch up to the power and influence of the SSE.) Later, Jiang Zemin ruled that, at least for the time being, China's stock exchanges would be limited to the SSE and SZSE, closing the door on other cities and municipalities hoping to follow in the footsteps of Shanghai and Shenzhen.

China's stock exchanges and, by extension, the Chinese capital market as a whole, could not have emerged were it not for the work of a few key officials and scholars, as well as the efforts of government agencies and commercial establishments.

On July 9, 1988, the PBC convened a securities market symposium at Beijing Wanshou Hotel. In attendance were officials from the Central Leading Group on Financial and Economic Affairs, the State Planning Commission, the State Commission for Economic Structural Reform, the PBC, the Ministry of Finance, and the Ministry of Foreign Trade and Economic Cooperation, as well as from state-run China Venturetech Investment Corporation (CVIC), China Agricultural Development Trust and Investment Corporation, and Kanghua Development Corporation. The symposium resulted in the formation of the "Stock Exchange Research and Design Team," under the organization of the PBC; Gong Zhuming, director of the PBC General Planning Department, CVIC president Zhang Xiaolin and others were charged with the task of drafting *Conception for Establishing and Regulating Stock Mar-*

kets in China. Additional reports, including *Proposal to Establish a National Securities Regulatory Commission* and *Basic Conception for Establishing Securities Law*, were also drafted during the symposium.

On March 15, 1989, nine organizations, including China International Trust and Investment Company (now the CITIC Group), China Everbright International Trust and Investment Company and

CVIC, each contributed 500,000 yuan to establish the Joint Office for Securities Market Research and Design of China—an organization famous throughout China's capital market circles and often abbreviated in Chinese as *Lianban*. Its name was later changed to the "Stock Exchange Executive Council" (SEEC). Gong Zhuming assumed the position of director-general, while Gao Xiqing, who had returned to China after working at the Wall Street law firm of Mudge Rose Guthrie Alexander & Ferdon, became lead counsel.

Although Lianban's initial idea of establishing a stock exchange in Beijing ran aground following the political incident of 1989, the notion of setting up a securities market received the strong support of China's central leadership. The SZSE and SSE were eventually opened, with Lianban as the sponsoring organization for both exchanges.

On December 2, 1989, Zhu Rongji, who, at the time, simultaneously held positions as Shanghai CPC Municipal Committee Secretary and Mayor of Shanghai, convened and chaired a financial reform conference at the Municipal Party committee assembly hall on Kangping Road. Li Xiangrui (Chairman of the Board of the Bank of Communications), Gong Haocheng (President of the Shanghai Branch of the PBC) and He Gaosheng (Director of the Shanghai Office for Economic Restructuring) were charged with forming the "Shanghai Stock Exchange Preparatory Group," of which Lianban's Zhang Zhifang was invited to assume the role of vice-leader. Under the prompt and resolute guidance of Zhu Rongji, the SSE was declared open for business one year later.

At the time, however, China's stock market was not only immature but, due to ideological influences, also suffered from numerous loopholes and potential future calamities. One example is the issue of "state-owned shares" and "legal-person shares," a problem unique to China's securities markets. The prevailing understanding of economic structural reform among ideological and theoretical circles in China in the 1980s led to the belief that a stock market should utilize the positive achievements of capitalist production methods while maintaining public ownership as its base. The development of China's shareholding system, therefore,

would require that the state controlled a majority stake of shares (or that a "whole-people-owned" or "collectively-owned" entity held a controlling stake). Furthermore, in order to prevent the loss of state-owned assets and maintain a controlling interest, these shares could not be listed or circulated.

During the pilot-listing of Chinese enterprises, large- and medium-sized SOEs were basically off-limits and only relatively small companies were listed. For instance, the first eight companies listed in China, known as Shanghai's *Laobagu* ("Old Eight Stocks"), consisted solely of neighborhood factories and township-and-village enterprises, with the exception of one electric vacuum maker (known as Shanghai Zhenkong Electronics). It was not until 1992 that Shanghai's pilot-listing initiative was expanded, with about 30 companies listed that year. In 1993, listing was further expanded to include companies all around China.

Thereafter, China's capital market continued to open and expand. By the end of 2007, after 18 years of development, Chinese enterprises had altogether raised 1.9 trillion yuan through the issuance of shares and transferable bonds, and the number of listed companies had grown to 1,550, with an aggregate market value of 32.71 trillion yuan—equivalent to 140 percent of GDP. Over the years, China's capital market has promoted the growth of China's economy and enterprises, sparked the reform of enterprise systems, stimulated change in the management model for SOEs and state-owned assets, accelerated the development of privately-owned enterprises and, ultimately, evolved to become an increasingly important part of the Chinese economy.

In this sense, no matter how many trials and hardships the future may hold, the establishment of China's capital market—and its operation to the present day—is, in and of itself, a great achievement in China's economic restructuring and reform.

21. The Introduction of "Nine Provisions of the State Council"

On January 31, 2004, the first Saturday since markets reopened after the Spring Festival holiday, *Some Opinions of the State Council on Promoting the Reform, Opening and Steady Growth of Capital Markets* (hereafter referred to as "Nine Provisions of the State Council") was issued. This short document of only 5,000 words has been called "a milestone in the development of China's securities market" for its far-reaching impact on subsequent market construction and policy orientation. On the first trading day after *Nine Provisions of the State Council* was issued, the SSE (Shanghai Stock Exchange) Composite Index rose 33 points from the previous day's closing of 1,590, ending the day at 1,623 points for

a gain of 2.08 percent.

The enactment of *Nine Provisions of the State Council* had an undeniably stimulatory effect on China's securities market. In 2001, as a result of the launch of the state-owned share reduction scheme, the market capitalization of China's securities market plummeted 342.7 billion yuan and, in 2002, fell another 320.9 billion yuan. In 2003, the market became even more crisis-ridden and the downward trend caused large numbers of investors to unload their stocks. The market's listlessness set one new record after another.

In September 2003, in particular, the notion that the Chinese stock market had become "marginalized" sparked a resurgence of debate and discussion on China's securities market. The China Securities Regulatory Commission (CSRC) was reproached by investors for its "governance by non-interference" and its "ostrich policy." In fact, in order to resolve the many difficulties that China's macroeconomy was experiencing at the time, the securities market would have to tackle its own list of problems: ever-growing insurance funds that required a larger number of and more robust investment channels; over-reliance on overseas markets in the restructuring and public listing of large state-owned enterprises and state-owned commercial banks directly relevant to the national economy

and people's livelihood; a lack of exit routes for venture investments; and the financing difficulties of small- and medium-sized enterprises.

Decision of the CPC Central Committee on Issues regarding the Improvement of the Socialist Market Economic System, passed at the Third Plenary Session of the 16th CCCPC on October 14, 2003, declared the Party's resolve to "vigorously develop capital and other factor markets and to actively promote the reform, opening and steady growth of capital markets." Guided by this approach, the CSRC set out to prepare the preliminary draft of the *Nine Provisions of the State Council*.

In November 2003, copies of *Some Opinions of the State Council on Promoting the Reform, Opening and Steady Growth of Capital Markets (Revised Exposure Draft)* were sent to the People's Bank of China, the China Banking Regulatory Commission, the China Insurance Regulatory Commission, the Ministry of Finance, and the State-owned Assets Supervision and Administration Commission of the State Council (SASAC) to solicit their opinions. In December, CSRC vice-chairman Tu Guangshao convened the aforesaid agencies and held two discussions to consolidate the suggested revisions of each department and submit them to the State Council

after reaching a consensus.

For Shang Fulin, who was appointed in 2003 as the fifth chairman of the CSRC, *Nine Provisions of the State Council* not only was his first achievement since taking up his new post, but also became the foundation upon which the "split-share structure" issue was ultimately resolved. Zhou Xiaochuan, the previous CSRC chairman, had tried to solve the problem once and for all by reducing state share ownership and, on June 12, 2001, a state-owned share reduction policy was adopted by the State Council. The policy was met by the collective resistance of the market and rescinded after being in effect for only three months—the first such embarrassment in the securities history of modern China.

After taking office, Shang Fulin opened a dialogue with all sides. He also enlisted the help of the previous CSRC chairman and other "higher-ups" to mediate between all parties. As the trend towards an increasingly depressed and marginalized capital market continued, all sides finally reached a basic common understanding. One of the most significant outcomes of this consensus of opinion was *Nine Provisions of the State Council*.

Nine Provisions of the State Council elevated China's goal to "vigorously develop capital markets," laying out a strategy to achieve the strategic target of quadrupling the national economy in the first 20 years of the 21st century. The nine provisions comprehensively and systematically set forth a series of nine important issues, in-

cluding the significance and guiding principles of capital market development; policies needing to be perfected; the construction of a capital market system; standardized operations of listed companies; the service quality of intermediary agencies; the level of market supervision; the prevention and elimination of risks; and the opening-up of capital markets.

The issuance of *Nine Provisions of the State Council* also marked the second time that China's highest administrative body had issued an official document to guide the reform and development of China's capital market. (The first such document was *Notice of the State Council on Further Strengthen-*

ing the Macro-management of Securities Markets, approved on December 17, 1992.) In addition, it marked the first time that the central government provided a comprehensive and categorical description of the function, guiding principles and task of developing the Chinese capital market.

During several subsequent stock-market slumps, *Nine Provisions of the State Council* was shown to have a calming effect on investors and the market. The debate about China's economic overheating that had broken out earlier in 2003 ultimately resulted in the full-scale launch of "macroeconomic regulation and control" by the central government on April 28, 2004.

Another far-reaching breakthrough of the *Nine Provisions of the State Council* with respect to China's securities markets was that it addressed, for the first time, the need to effectively protect the lawful rights and interests of investors, especially public investors. This indicated that China's leadership had recognized the important position of public investors in capital markets and thus, through policymaking, provided a self-defence weapon for holders of tradable shares. At the same time, *Nine Provisions of the State Council* awakened the consciousness of holders of tradable shares and raised their awareness about protecting their own rights and interests.

22. Tax Revenue-sharing System Reform

In 1992, the report to the 14th National Congress of the CPC pointed out that China "should gradually implement a separation of tax and profit and a tax revenue-sharing system"; the same year, the central government selected Tianjin and eight other regions as pilot sites for the tax revenue-sharing system. In 1993, at the Third Plenary Session of the 14th CCCPC, reform of the tax revenue-sharing system was formally written into *Resolution on Several Important Issues Pertaining to the Socialist Market Economy*.

Everyone who has read historian Ray Huang's book *1587, A Year of No Significance* should realize that, evidently, this was not merely a financial reform. As CPC General Secretary Jiang Zemin

noted in his speech: "The goal of implementing a tax revenue-sharing system, rationally dividing the duties and responsibilities of the central and local governments, and equitably determining the ratio of revenue and expenditure between the central and local governments is to harmonize economic relations and standardize economic activities... This not only conforms to common international practice, but also takes account of China's special characteristics and specific conditions. In this way, we can bring into full play the initiative of both the central and the local authorities." Jiang further added: "When dealing with relations between the central and local governments, the central government must consider the difficulties of localities, and localities must establish the notion of the whole. The whole takes care of the part, and the part submits to the whole."

During the late 1980s and early 1990s, China's state finances fell into a severe crisis; because of rapid declines in the ratio of government revenue to GDP and the ratio of central to total gov-

ernment revenue, the central government faced a state of unprecedented weakness. The central government's weakened financial capacity resulted in a major shortage of construction funds for national defence, basic research and other essential undertakings that required national government funding.

When China held its national finance meeting in 1991, central government finances were in bad shape. Given the large budget deficits, it appeared that planning the next year's budget was not going to be an easy task. Left with no other choice, then Minister of Finance Wang Bingqian asked each province to make a "contribution" (ranging from 10 to 100 million yuan), effectively turning the national finance meeting into an impromptu fundraiser. Wang's "panhandling," however, was promptly and mercilessly rejected by the directors of China's regional finance departments. The finance directors of some of the wealthier provinces even got into vehement quarrels with Wang, their own highest-ranking superior.

By 1993, the troubles of China's state finances had only escalated. Wang Bingqian gave the following example: In the first quarter of 1993, total government revenue fell by 2.2 percent from the same period one year prior, while GDP rose by 15.1 percent in the first quarter of 1993. A serious imbalance had emerged in the relative proportions of government revenue and economic growth. For mandatory spending, however, which required the funding of the

central government revenue, not a cent (or *fen*) could be spared.

On July 23, 1993, Zhu Rongji, then vice-premier of the State Council, arrived at the national finance and taxation working meeting. Speaking to top officials of China's regional finance departments, Zhu cautioned: "Under the current system, central government finances are in bad shape. If we do not reform now, the days of central finance will be numbered." He pointed out that, in developed market-economy countries, the ratio of central government revenues to total government revenues is generally 60 percent or above, while the ratio of central government expenditures to total government expenditures is about 40 percent. At the time, China's case was the exact opposite: central government revenues occupied less than 40 percent of total government revenues, while central expenditures constituted over 50 percent of total government expenditures.

It was this financial crisis that led the central government to undertake far-reaching reforms in the tax revenue-sharing system. During the course of tax revenue-sharing reform, the Third Plenary Session of the 14th CPC Central Committee played a decisive role. In 1994, the reforms were fully and officially implemented. Under the new tax revenue-sharing scheme, the 1993 local tax revenues were taken as a base amount and each region was promised that this amount would be returned in full. Value-added tax was shared between the central and local governments according to a ratio of 75:25, providing local governments an incentive to increase tax revenues.

Since the founding of New China in 1949, the country's financial system has undergone several major reforms. During the early years of the PRC, a former Soviet Union-style centralized system

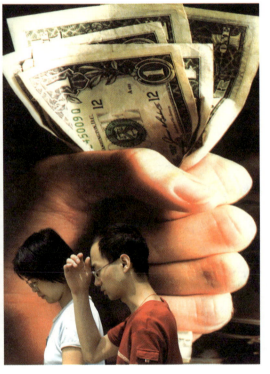

of tax revenue collection and distribution was carried out for 20 years in a row. In 1980, China began to implement a system of decentralized power (the scheme of "eating from separate stoves"). In 1988, this was superseded by a multiform management system known as the "contract responsibility system." In practice, however, none of these reforms were able to break through the public finance framework of China's planned economy. In 1994, the country's economic conditions finally forced the government to take a revolutionary step toward creating a market economic system, i.e., a move from administrative to economic decentralization.

In the 14 years since its implementation, China's tax revenue-sharing system has

achieved great success. Many economists have noted that the 1994 reforms solidified the central government's ability to concentrate on carrying out major tasks (especially abolishing agricultural tax and strengthening investment in social security, education and scientific research) for over a decade thereafter. From 1993 to 2007, central government revenue rose from 95.7 billion yuan to 2.7739 trillion yuan, a gain of 2,899 percent. Local governments, too, had a strong incentive to develop their economies. Over the same 14-year span, total local government revenues increased from 339.1 billion yuan to 2.3565 trillion yuan.

Starting in 2005, renewed calls were made to further ameliorate China's financial and taxation system reforms, with a focus on the tax revenue-sharing system. In 2007, the 17th National Congress of the CPC resolved to carry forward its financial and taxation system reform plan, under the guidance of the Scientific Outlook on Development.

23. Thirty Years of SOE Reform

The *Decision of the CPC Central Committee on Issues regarding the Establishment of a Socialist Market Economic System*, passed at the Third Plenary Session of the 14th CCCPC in November 1993, stated that in order to establish a socialist market economic system, China "must resolutely maintain the dominance of public ownership; further transform the management mechanisms of state-owned enterprises; and establish a modern enterprise system that can adapt to the needs of the market economy and that has clearly defined property rights, clearly specified powers and responsibilities, separation of government and enterprise, and scientific management." After carrying out experimental reforms in the contract system, leasing

system, asset management responsibility system and shareholding system, China's top policymakers for the first time affirmed and defined the direction of SOE reform, sounding a "bugle call" to set the comprehensive reform of SOEs in motion.

As the name suggests, "state-owned enterprise reform" entails reforms at both the state and enterprise level. While enterprise reform has involved internal reforms of the enterprises themselves, state-level reform has targeted the lack of separation between government and enterprises left over from the traditional state-owned system; this included making substantive and significant reforms in and adjustments to the relationship between government and enterprises in accordance with the basic requirements of building a socialist market economy.

Reforming the state, reforming the lack of separation between government and enterprises, and making substantive and significant reforms in and adjustments to the relationship between the state and enterprises thus became the essence of, and the key to, SOE reform. Only by understanding this essence could an effec-

tive foundation for SOE reform be established. To this end, China has made unremitting efforts towards SOE reform since the reform and opening-up initiative was first launched in 1978.

SOE reform can be roughly divided into five phases. The first phase was from late-1978 to September 1984. This was the pilot phase for expanding enterprise autonomy. During this phase, the government conferred on enterprises various powers in the areas of plan formulation, product sales and retained earnings. In particular, the implementation of a system of retained profits gave SOEs a certain amount of financial power to advance production, improve collective employee welfare, and offer incentives and rewards to employees, thereby enhancing the vitality of these enterprises.

The second phase of SOE reform was from October 1984 to the end of 1986. During this phase, multiple modes of operation, with the contract system playing a dominant role, were implemented. In October 1984, the Third Plenary Session of the 12th CCCPC passed *Resolution of the CPC Central Committee on Reform of the Economic System*, launching China's urban economic system reform. The focus of this phase of SOE reform was on the separation of government and enterprises, the separation of ownership and management rights, and the implementation of multiple modes of business operation. The majority of enterprises adopted the contract responsibility system as their mode of operation. There were several different forms of contract. Some small-scale enterprises implemented a leasing management system,

while only a minority of enterprises adopted the pilot joint-stock reform program. With the arrival of multiple management modes, the autonomy of China's enterprises had further expanded.

The third phase of SOE reform was from 1987 to late-1993. This was the phase during which enterprise management mechanisms were transformed. During this stage, the focus of enterprise reform shifted from the expansion of powers and the transfer of profits to transforming enterprise mechanisms, with the specific focus still on improving the contract responsibility system. To this end, the State Council issued *Provisional Regulations on the Contractual Management Responsibility System for Industrial Enterprises Owned by the Whole People* and *Enforcement Regulations on Enterprise Law* as well as *Regulations on Transforming the Operational Mechanism of Industrial Enterprises Owned by the Whole People*, which granted enterprises 14 rights of autonomous management. At the same

time, as a result of reductions in mandatory planning and continued price liberalization, many state-owned enterprises were pushed into the market and began operating according to market principles.

The fourth phase of SOE reform was from 1994 to early-2003. The focus of reform during this phase was on establishing a modern enterprise system. In November 1993, *Decision of the CPC Central Committee on Issues regarding the Establishment of a Socialist Market Economic System* was passed at the Third Plenary Session of the 14th CCCPC. The document clearly stated the new direction of China's SOE reform: to build a modern enterprise system with "clearly defined property rights, clearly specified powers and responsibilities, separation of government and enterprises, and scientific management" and that could adapt to the needs of the market economy. Around the same time, the NPC issued *Enterprise Law*, signifying that China's SOE reform had entered the phase of establishing a modern enterprise system and achieving enterprise system innovation.

The fifth phase of SOE reform began on April 6, 2003, on which day the SASAC was founded, and has continued to the present day. During this phase, the policy of "seizing the large and abandoning the small" (retaining and nurturing large SOES while privatizing small ones) was implemented, enabling China to "reduce its battlefront." Many SOEs have been successfully transformed into joint stock businesses, and, under the supervision of SASAC, the remaining SOEs have achieved rapid development. By the end of 2007, the number of SOEs had contracted from tens of thousands at the outset of reforms to just over 150; total assets soared from several hundred billion yuan to 14.6 trillion yuan; and annual profits had increased from a few billion yuan to 980 billion yuan. China's "central enterprises" (i.e., large-scale SOEs under the direct management of the central government) have become the largest national competitive entities in the world.

Since the onset of China's reform era, SOE reform efforts have achieved great success. This SOE reform initiative, however, remains a work in progress. Whether divested SOEs, as former adjuncts to the state government, can truly become independent economic entities (and market-competitive entities) ultimately depends on whether implementation of the reform policy to separate government and enterprises is complete and thorough; and whether all important powers pertaining to human, financial and material resources, management, and other intra-enterprise elements and processes are placed inside, rather than outside, the enterprise.

24. The Launch of Banking Reform

2004 was an important year in China's financial development history. That year, reform of state-owned commercial banks finally entered a "substantive" phase, as the restructuring of China Construction Bank and Bank of China into joint-stock commercial

banks began. This much anticipated "reform train" raced out of the station, with a speed and momentum unsurpassed by any period in history.

In fact, over the course of

the preceding 10 years, reform of China's state-owned commercial banks had been continuously underway. The reforms prior to 2004 can be roughly divided into two phases:

1984 to 1994: Specialization reform. Prior to 1984, China had maintained a unified (one-tier) banking system. In 1984, against the backdrop of reform and opening-up, Industrial and Commercial Bank of China, China Construction Bank, Agricultural Bank of China and Bank of China were spun off from People's Bank of China as specialized state banks, while People's Bank of China took on the exclusive role of China's central bank. This marked the birth of China's two-tier banking system, with each tier responsible for its own functions.

1994 to 2003: Reform of wholly state-owned commercial banks. In 1994, China established three "policy banks," achieving a separation of policy finance and commercial finance. In 1995, *Commercial Bank Law of the People's Republic of China* was issued and implemented. The law defined state-owned commercial banks as market entities that "operate autonomously, take responsibility for their own risks, assume sole responsibility for their profits and losses, and exercise self-restraint." Prior to that point, China's four specialized banks had been legally defined as wholly state-owned commercial banks. In 1997, the Asian financial crisis erupted. In November of that year, the central government convened China's first "National Financial Working Conference," after which a series of reform measures for China's state-owned commercial banks were rolled out. During this phase, many advanced concepts and methods were introduced, while exter-

nal administrative intervention was reduced significantly. For the most part, however, the reforms of this phase involved surface-level matters—such as maintaining strong relations between banks and the government, introducing advanced management technology, and disposing of non-performing assets—and had not yet touched upon institutional and other deeper-level issues.

Given this state of affairs, the State Council decided in late-2003 to approve the establishment of Central Huijin Investment Corporation (hereafter "Huijin"), marking a new round of even more aggressive banking reform. On behalf of the government, the state-owned Huijin injected US$45 billion of the country's foreign exchange reserves into Bank of China and China Construction Bank (US$22.5 billion each). As the financier, Huijin also supervised and expedited the work of the two banks to ensure that they carried out every measure of the reform program and to effect improvements in the banks' corporate gover-

nance structure.

China's banking reform proceeded under the principle of "one bank, one policy." In addition to Bank of China and China Construction Bank, Industrial and Commercial Bank of China and Agricultural Bank of China also completed each step in the process of capital injection, restructuring and listing in accordance with reform requirements. From the outset, the reform adopted the approach of addressing both cause and symptoms. As financial restructuring got underway, China Banking Regulatory Commission (CBRC) specially issued *Guidance on the Corporate Governance Reform and Supervision of Bank of China and China Construction Bank*, establishing a ten-point program for corporate governance structure reform. Three categories and seven evaluative criteria were established, and strict assessments of the two pilot banks were carried out on a quarterly basis.

The first banks to carry out this series of dynamic reforms were China Construction Bank and Bank of China, which attracted Bank of America and Royal Bank of Scotland, respectively, as strategic investors. In October 2005 and June 2006, respectively, China Construction Bank and Bank of China were listed on the Hong Kong Stock Exchange. The joint-stock reform of Industrial and Commercial Bank of China soon followed; in October 2006, it was simultaneously listed in both Shanghai and Hong Kong through the issuance of A-shares and H-shares, respectively. Although Agricultural Bank of China has yet to be listed, plans to effect its transformation into a public company are still underway.

Following the reforms, the three listed commercial banks took on a brand-new look. The banks' capital adequacy ratio, asset quality, earning power and other financial indices showed marked improvements over their pre-reform levels, and fundamental progress was seen in financial performance. The banks also employed the financial backing of strategic investors to develop new business, enhance financial innovation, and improve the quality of financial services. Two of the listed banks, Industrial and Commercial Bank of China and China Construction Bank, set up fund management companies on a pilot basis. In accordance with the requirements of regulatory authorities, the banks partnered with internationally renowned institutions to establish a Sino-for-

eign joint-venture fund management company, which has since successfully commenced the sale of fund products.

The successful listing of three large state-owned commercial banks is by no means the end of China's banking reform. The focus of Chinese banking reforms has shifted to small- and medium-sized joint-stock commercial banks with nationwide operating licenses, as well as municipal commercial banks with regional operating licenses. For the most part, their reform model will follow the three-step formula of restructuring, capital-raising and listing. Since China Construction Bank, Bank of China, and Industrial and Commercial Bank of China were first listed, their profits and financial statuses have been stronger and more stable than at any other time in history, and their operational capabilities have become internationally competitive. The listing of banks on stock exchanges, however, is not the ultimate goal of China's banking reform. Banking reform is an arduous, complex and long-term process, and the results that China has achieved to date represent the completion of only the preliminary stages of reforms.

25. China's New Dream: Building a Harmonious Society

In the course of five millennia of Chinese ideological history, the ideology of a "harmonious society" emerged early on in the Confucian and Taoist classics.

2,500 years ago, the philosopher Confucius advanced the social ideal of a "World of Great Unity" (*Datong Shijie*). Confucius held that, in our interpersonal relations, we should emphasize honesty and good faith, strive for benevolence and amicability, coexist in harmony, and treat others equally; and that society should employ the able, promote the worthy, and strive for affluence and good health. It was believed that, in this way, a society of peace, harmony and auspiciousness could be created. Over two thousand years later, the late-Qing reformer Kang Youwei, in his book

Datong Shu (literally "Book of Great Unity"), advocated the building of an ideal society in which "everyone loves everyone else, everyone is equal and the whole world is one community."

The "World of Great Unity" advocated in traditional Chinese culture was, in fact, a dream of the ancient people to build a society imbued with harmony. This beautiful image, a blueprint for a harmonious socialist society, emerged before the Chinese people.

In October 2006, the *Resolution of the CPC Central Committee on Major Issues Regarding the Building of a Harmonious Socialist Society* (hereafter referred to as "Resolution on Building a Harmonious Society") was passed at the Sixth Plenary Session of the 16th CCCPC. At the plenum, the CPC Central Committee stressed the need "to place the building of a harmonious socialist society in a more prominent position" as China enters a new century and a new stage of development.

This was the first time that a CPC document had placed the building of a harmonious society in a prominent position alongside economic, political and cultural construction. The objective of "building a well-off society in an all-around way" and "building socialism with Chinese characteristics" was thus expanded from a three-part scheme—i.e., developing the socialist market economy, socialist democracy, and advanced socialist culture—into a four-part scheme that added "building a harmonious socialist society" to the list. In addition, it was the first time since the beginning of China's reform and opening-up era that social construction was

the main topic of discussion at a Party Central Committee plenary session. The *Resolution on Building a Harmonious Society* is regarded as the first guiding document on strengthening social construction since the Communist Party assumed power in 1949. With this document, "improving the ability to build a harmonious socialist society" was advanced as an important factor in the Party's capacity to govern.

In short, a "harmonious socialist society" is a society in which each component and element of the social structure exists in a state of mutual harmony. With respect to what constitutes a "harmonious society," people of different eras have had different understanding and awareness. Both the Utopian society described by the ancient Greek philosopher Plato in *The Republic* and ancient China's "society of great unity" represent the ideal "harmo-

nious society" envisioned and embraced by past eras. The attainment of this ideal, however, is by no means an overnight process.

During the early years of China's reform, although the CPC did not advance the goal of building a harmonious society, it did pay attention to the coordinated development of economic, political, cultural and other socialist undertakings. The Party promoted the strategic policy of "grasping with two hands" (i.e., a dual focus on achieving economic growth and strengthening political power), thus laying the foundation on which to build a harmonious society.

As China stepped into the 21st century, the questions of how to resolve conflicts and issues that would arise as China progressed and how to achieve better and faster economic development became the Party's top concerns. The first time that the concept of "building a harmonious socialist society" was comprehensively advanced was at the Fourth Plenary Session of the 16th CCCPC on September 19, 2004. Subsequently, an extensive publicity campaign and the launch and gradual implementation of a series of concrete policy measures made the meaning of the "harmonious society" concept clearer with each day. Gradually, this concept engendered the common understanding and the shared desire of all society.

In 2005, the CPC advanced the objective of building a "harmonious society" as the Party's strategic task; this concept of "harmony" thus became the value orientation for the process of build-

ing "socialism with Chinese characteristics." On February 19, 2005, the CCCPC convened a seminar in Beijing with major provincial- and ministerial-level leaders on the subject of "improving the ability to build a harmonious socialist society." For the first time, CPC General Secretary Hu Jintao fully expounded the meaning of a "harmonious society," defining it as a society typified by "democracy and law; fairness and justice; integrity and friendship; vigor and vitality; stability and order; and the harmonious coexistence of man and nature."

On March 5, the opening day of the Third Session of the 10th NPC, Premier Wen Jiabao specially devoted an entire chapter in the government work report to elaborating concrete policy mea-

sures aimed at building a harmonious society.

In November 2006, after a year of preparatory work, "building a harmonious society" was finally placed on the agenda at the Sixth Plenary Session of the 16th CCCPC. The plenum report proclaimed: "A harmonious socialist society is both a society full of vigor and a society of unity and harmony. We must stimulate the energy of society to its full; promote  the harmony of relationships between political parties, ethnic groups, religions, social strata, and compatriots at home and abroad; strengthen the great unity of the people of all ethnic groups; and enhance the great solidarity of all the sons and daughters of the Chinese nation at home and overseas."

26. The Non-public Economy: A "Major Component"

On March 15, 1999, *Amendments to the Constitution of the People's Republic of China* was passed at the Second Session of the Ninth NPC. The most striking change in this revision of China's fundamental law was the following: "Individual, private and other non-public sectors of the economy that exist within the limits prescribed by law are major components of the socialist market economy." From its prior status as a "necessary and beneficial supplement" to becoming a "major component," China's non-public economy had overcome a series of structural and ideological hurdles and, for the first time in the history of the country's legal system, had extricated itself from the embarrassment of hav-

ing a vaguely acknowledged non-public economy.

By this time, about 33 percent of China's industrial output value was derived from the non-public economy (including the individual private sector); retail sales of consumer goods in the non-public sector stood at 51.5 percent of total consumer goods retail sales; and tax revenue accounted for 10 percent of total government revenues. Having become an important constituent of the Chinese economy, the non-public sector could finally "hold its head high" and gain the respect it deserved.

According to Gu Shengzu, vice-chairman of the All-China Federation of Industry and Commerce, China's nearly 30-year-long period of non-public economic development was one of ideological emancipation and theoretical innovation, comprising an arduous process of learning and experience. Each successive Congress of the CPC gained new insight into the non-public economy and made important theoretical breakthroughs. Subsequently, each theoretical leap forward and each new system reform opened up a broad space for development, providing a theo-

retical and policy foundation upon which the non-public economy could develop and grow.

During this period, China's non-public economy achieved three breakthroughs. The first one was its transformation from being the "tail of capitalism" to a "necessary and beneficial supplement." Prior to 1978, the non-public economy was considered "the tail of capitalism," a tail that leaders demanded be "cut off." In 1982, the report to the 12th National Congress of the CPC repositioned the non-public economy as "a necessary and beneficial supplement" to the public economy. A decade later, in 1992, the 14th National Congress of the CPC called for "the joint long-term development of multiple economic elements, led by China's public ownership system (including ownership by the whole people and collective ownership) and supplemented by the individual, private, and foreign-funded sectors." During this phase, the non-public economy broke through the ideological "forbidden zone"; the individual economy achieved rapid development and the private economy gained recognition.

The second breakthrough was a redefinition of the non-public sector's role from a "necessary and beneficial supplement" to the public economy to a "major component" of the socialist market economy. The 1997 report to the 15th National Congress of the CPC positioned the non-public sector as a "major component" of China's socialist market economy. In doing so, the report effected a transformation of the non-public economy from an inorganic,

external "supplement" into an internal "major component." In comparison to the public economy, however, the non-public sector remained relatively confined and many restrictions were still placed on its development.

The third breakthrough, as indicated in the 2002 report to the 16th National Congress of the CPC and the 2007 report to the 17th National Congress of the CPC, was the transformation of the non-public sector from a "major component" of the socialist market economy into a market entity that enjoys equal "national treatment." The report to the 16th National Congress of the CPC stated: "[We] must unwaveringly consolidate and develop the public sector of the economy and unwaveringly encourage, support and guide the development of the non-public sector. [We] must uphold the leading role of the public economy, promote the development of the non-public economy, and integrate both into the course of socialist modernization construction." These two "unwavering" points and one "integration" paved

the way for the development, at the basic system level, of the non-public economy.

Five years later, the report to the 17th National Congress of the CPC went another step further, stating: "[We] must unwaveringly consolidate and develop the public sector of the economy and unwaveringly encourage, support and guide the development of the non-public sector. [We] must ensure equal protection of property rights and create a new condition in which all economic sectors compete on an equal footing and serve to reinforce each other." The "two equals" philosophy ("equal protection" under law and "equal competition" in economic activities) became the highlight of the 17th CPC National Congress's treatment of non-public economic theory.

On February 25, 2005, the State Council issued *Some Opinions on Encouraging, Supporting and Guiding the Development of the Non-Public Economy*; this was the central government's first document on promoting development of the non-public economy since the PRC was founded in 1949. Because the document contains 36 regulations, it is also known as the "36 Regulations on the Non-Public Economy." The document allows non-public capital to enter monopolized industries and fields. In addition, it stipulates that no entity or individual may infringe upon the lawful property of non-public enterprises or unlawfully alter the property ownership rights of such enterprises.

In reality, all of these theoretical breakthroughs were founded on the rapid development and increasingly important position of

the non-public economy. From 1978 to 2006, a span of less than 30 years, the non-public sector's share of GDP increased from 0.9 percent to over 40 percent, an average annual growth rate of over 25 percent—significantly higher than the country's average annual GDP growth rate of 9 percent over the same period. Since the mid-1990s, especially, the non-public economy has been responsible for providing over 70 percent of new urban jobs, and for employing more than 70 percent of migrant laborers.

The most unique feature of China's first 30 years of reform has been the gradual path of expanding the "increment" before adjusting the "stock" and of moving from "extra-systemic" reforms to "intra-systemic" reforms. While maintaining a streamlined state-owned economy, China has strived to vigorously develop the non-public sector and cultivate the market economy, thus forming an effective and competitive market environment in which market power permeates the system to "force" intra-systemic reforms. The result of these efforts is the vibrant market economy driven by pluralistic competition and common development that China enjoys today. With respect to this point, the non-public sector has rendered outstanding service.

27. China's "No-devaluation" Pledge

On March 17, 1998, during the "Two Sessions" (the Chinese People's Political Consultative Conference and the sessions of the NPC), as the Asian financial crisis continued to wreak havoc, newly elected State Council premier Zhu Rongji announced China's new "One Assurance" policy: "We must ensure that China's economic growth rate reaches 8 percent and that the inflation rate stays below 3 percent. We will not de-

value the renminbi." This was the second time that Zhu Rongji, on behalf of the Chinese government, had publicly pledged not to devalue the renminbi, instantly attracting the close attention of the world market.

After the Asian financial crisis erupted in the summer of 1997, the renminbi became the focus of attention in the global financial sector. With many Asian countries undergoing relentless currency depreciation and steadily declining imports, it would not be easy for China to maintain its no-devaluation pledge. In order to survive the Asian financial crisis, Japan—which owned the world's largest foreign exchange reserves at the time—devalued its currency for three years in a row. Singapore and Taiwan, likewise, devalued their respective currencies to strengthen export competitiveness and protect domestic job opportunities. Given the intensely competitive international market, currency devaluation could even have been considered an understandable action. All the while, many people were skeptical of China's pledge not to devalue the renminbi.

In 1997, investor and financial speculator George Soros dealt severe economic blows to several Southeast Asian countries (none of which proved to be his match), before turning his aim towards China. Given China's position as one of the most important economies of Asia, the fall of the renminbi would have exacerbated the already desperate plight of the entire Asian region. In late-October 1997, World Bank held its annual meeting in Hong Kong, with Soros, then Malaysian prime minister Mahathir bin Mohamad, and then Russian vice-premier Anatoly Chubais in attendance. The

question of whether the renminbi would be devalued became the meeting's most sensitive and important subject of discussion.

On October 22, 1997, speaking at a lecture specially organized on his behalf by World Bank, Zhu Rongji offered China's first public pledge not to devalue its currency: "China will adhere to its position not to devalue the renminbi and will take on the historic responsibility of stabilizing Asia's economic environment." As soon as this statement was made, leaders attending from across Asia breathed a deep sigh of relief. *Far Eastern Economic Review* remarked: "This is the first

time that China, during a global economic crisis, has revealed its graceful demeanor as an economic power."

In contrast to the Chinese people's rock-solid trust in Zhu Rongji, international speculators had by no means cast away their doubts about China's no-devaluation pledge. Japan, which at the time was much more economically robust than China, had let the yen lose value in attempts to shift its economic troubles onto its neighbors. As a result, stock and foreign exchange markets across Southeast Asia fell steadily, the region's financial markets experienced renewed turbulence, and Southeast Asian economies already hit hard by the financial crisis slid further downhill. At this point, the "battle-hungry" Soros opted to bypass China's controls on international capital transactions, and instead attack the Hong Kong dollar (HKD)—the currency most closely associated with the renminbi.

In the preceding years, the European and American mainstream media were already gloomy about Hong Kong's future after its return to Chinese sovereignty. To make matters worse, the territory was hit in January 1998 with an outbreak of bird flu, resulting in six deaths and prompting the slaughter of 1.3 million chickens. All of Hong Kong fell into a panic, and it was not

until half a year later that the epidemic finally abated. It was against this backdrop of turbulence and instability that Soros, on August 5, 1998, launched his "sniper attack" against the Hong Kong dollar.

Within a single day, international speculators dumped over 20 billion HKD. The Hong Kong Monetary Authority (HKMA) used its financial reserves to repurchase this amount in full, and fixed the exchange rate at 7.75 HKD/USD in order to stabilize the exchange market. The next day, speculators dumped another 20 billion HKD, and the HKMA again steeled itself and bought it all back. Six days later, speculators were still selling like crazy, and a battle of unprecedented intensity ensued between buyers and sellers. The Hang Seng Index plunged to 6,600 points, down almost 10,000 points from a year earlier. In total, about two trillion HKD of market value evaporated.

In mid-August 1998, backed by the support of Zhu Rongji and especially in light of the fact that the Chinese government was holding over US$140 billion in foreign reserves, the Hong Kong government threw its abundant foreign exchange funds into stock and futures markets to protect the Hong Kong dollar. After several rounds, Soros Group was finally defeated at the 4:00 pm closing bell on August 28. Steven Cheung, an economist at the University of Hong Kong, offered his insight: "No one who engages in financial derivatives trading is backed by endless capital support. As Soros pounded the HKD exchange rate, the Chinese government [supported and propped up Hong Kong.] In the end, the speculators were scared off."

To protect the renminbi from depreciation, the Chinese government took on unprecedented risks and endured unparalleled pressure. After being hit by the Asian financial crisis, China's consistently strong export growth began to decline, domestic merchandise inventory levels soared, and consumer demand became extremely sluggish. In June, the Yangtze River basin was hit by flooding of seldom-seen magnitude. Twenty-nine provinces and municipalities were affected by the flood, resulting in direct economic loss of 255.1 billion yuan. By this time, the consensus of global opinion was clear: Unless the renminbi were devalued, the Chinese economy would find itself in a dangerous predicament.

Nevertheless, Zhu Rongji, representing the Chinese government, used his own method to demonstrate the independence and

uniqueness of the Chinese economy. By upholding his pledge not to devalue the renminbi, he also enabled the international community—and especially developed Western nations—to witness, for the first time, China's poise as a responsible world power. Speaking to this point, Margaret Thatcher, former British prime minister, offered her praise to China: "In the future, there will be two major world powers: one is the United States and the other is China."

Of course, most convinced of all were the countries that had been hit hardest by the Asian financial crisis. In a July 1998 interview, one prominent Thai economist offered the following praise: "That China's leaders made several pledges not to devalue the renminbi is extraordinary. China did not take advantage of others' misfortunes; it actively took on great difficulties and risks, and made sacrifices. China made invaluable contributions towards stabilizing the Asian economic order as well as stimulating the recovery and development of the Southeast Asian economy."

In fact, after 1998, the Chinese yuan not only avoided depreciation, but actually gained in value: the renminbi notes in the hands of the Chinese people were worth even more than before. Of course, the biggest "dividend" of all was that, by thwarting the renminbi's depreciation, China helped to maintain the orderly state of the Southeast Asian economy while enhancing the country's own economic repute at the same time.

28. "Three Represents" and Private Property Protection

March 14, 2004 was just another ordinary day. Beijing's weather had started to warm up, and the people were enjoying the warm and moist air of early spring. At five o'clock in the afternoon, following the closing session of the 10th NPC, Chinese premier Wen Jiabao spoke at a press conference in front of about 700 Chinese and foreign journalists.

A reporter from a German TV station was the seventh journalist to rise and ask a question. The question concerned the amended Constitution and its enforcement. Wen Jiabao replied: "This constitutional amendment is of great significance to China's development. Leading officials of the Communist Party of China

and all Party members will play an exemplary role in abiding by it."

Wen's reply may have seemed like a simple answer to a simple question. One of the most important issues under discussion at the 2004 NPC session, however, was the introduction of the fourth amendment to China's 1982 Constitution. In addition to conferring constitutional status to Jiang Zemin's "Three Represents" ideology, the protection of human rights and private property were also, for the first time, written into the Constitution, and attracted a great deal of attention. On March 2, three days before the 2004 NPC session had even begun, the Associated Press announced to the world: "This is the first such action for China since its liberation in 1949."

Just prior to the press conference on that March 14 afternoon, the Constitution Amendment Bill had been adopted by NPC deputies with an overwhelming majority of 2,863 votes in favor, 10 against, and 17 abstentions. This seemingly simple and effortless attainment, however, was in actuality the product of 26 years of hardship, the culmination of three generations' efforts, and the realization of the aspirations of over one billion Chinese citizens.

For quite a long period of time after the founding of the PRC in 1949, the Chinese people embraced the commune system—characterized as "large in size and collective in nature" (i.e., large-scale enterprises under public ownership)—and did not dare to speak of wealth or riches. Even feeding a few chickens or raising a couple of sheep would have been considered "the tail of capitalism" and subsequently "cut off." The slogan "Give enough to the state, save enough for the collective, and the remainder belongs to the individual"—which emerged alongside the "all-around responsibility system" of rural Anhui in 1978—kicked off China's economic reform and ignited the Chinese people's long-suppressed desire to create wealth.

The singular socialist concept of public ownership was first "breached" in the countryside with the appearance of the rural "household responsibility system," which bore private property-like characteristics. At the same time, private industry and commerce, too, were bubbling in the undercurrent. Before long, the household workshops of Wenzhou (in Zhejiang Province), the small commodities trade of Shishi (in Fujian), and the processing industry of the Pearl River Delta had become renowned all across China.

When faced with a raging undercurrent, the most sensible approach is one of adaptation and guidance. In December 1978, two policy documents on agriculture were adopted at the Third Plenary Session of the 11th CCCPC, proclaiming a lift on the ban on rural industry and commerce, thus giving recognition to household sideline occupations and rural trade markets. In the spring of 1982, the central government fully affirmed the household contract responsibility system. The fourth Constitution of the PRC, passed on December 4, 1982, is regarded as the beginning of "the protection of private property to a limited extent" in China; the "private individual economy" was defined as "a supplement to the socialist public-ownership economy"; the term "private property" was defined in the Constitution as "lawfully earned income, savings and houses." In April 1988, the Constitution Amendment Bill was approved at the First

Session of the Seventh NPC, and the term "private economy" appeared in Chinese constitutional law for the first time. In June of the same year, the State Council issued *Provisional Regulations of the People's Republic of China on Private Enterprises*, finally giving formal recognition to China's private economy—and ending its almost 10-year-long history of obscurity and concealment.

The private economy thus entered a period of development and growth. At the end of 1989, industrial and commercial registration was implemented nationwide for the first time, and the number of registered private enterprises climbed to 90,600. Prior to this, only six private firms in all of China (four in Wenzhou and two in Shenyang) had obtained business licenses.

In fact, ever since the dawn of China's reform and opening-up initiative 30 years ago, citizens of all classes had begun to own "private property" (although it was not acknowledged as such until much later) in accord with their respective social statuses. Protection of this private property, therefore, was not only a matter for the wealthy, but inherently relevant to every citizen. Over the course of several years of development, China's private entrepreneurs also formed their own class—known by scholars as "the new rich class." The political spokesperson for this class of entrepreneurs, the All-China Federation of Industry and Commerce, submitted

three group motions, beginning with the 1998 "Two Sessions," to demand legislation for private property protection. The eager desire of China's private entrepreneurs soon condensed into a collective political appeal and began to enter the country's mainstream channels.

At the 1998 "Two Sessions," Zheng Zhuohui, a private entrepreneur from Shenzhen who had been elected for the first time as a deputy to the NPC, spent over three days trying to rally the support of the delegation of the Guangdong Provincial People's Congress. Finally, after securing the backing of 49 delegates, Zheng submitted an NPC resolution, in his own name, for "the protection of private property." This was the first individually filed bill calling for private property to be written into the Constitution.

With the ratification of the constitutional amendment on March 14, 2004, the "Three Represents" ideology was incorporated into the Constitution. The essence of this ideology is that the CPC not only represents the working class, but also represents the in-

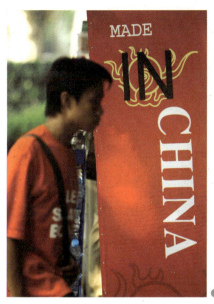

terests of the broad masses, including the interests of private entrepreneurs. The term "broad masses" also encompasses the new stratum of "socialist builders" associated with the non-public economy. With the guarantee that "citizens' lawful private property is inviolable" written into the Constitution, the property rights issue that had long perplexed China's entrepreneurs was finally and thoroughly resolved.

In March 2007, *Property Law of the People's Republic of China (Draft)*, the specific bill put forward to carry through the Constitutional clause that "citizens' lawful private property is inviolable," was passed into effect. The law affirmed the concept and legislative spirit of equal protection of all forms of property. For the first time, China placed personal property on an equal legal footing with state property.

29. China's "New Countryside" Campaign

The *Proposal of the CCCPC for Formulating the 11th Five-Year Plan for National Economic and Social Development*, passed at the Fifth Plenary Session of the 16th CCCPC in October 2005, stated for the first time that "building a new socialist countryside is a major historic task in China's modernization drive." Proceeding from reality and heeding the wishes of the peasants, China set out to execute the stable construction of a "new countryside."

The implementation of a reform policy should not be a superficial display of smoke and mirrors but rather a robust series of institutional innovations. The problems facing agriculture, rural areas and farmers have always been major issues that affect China's overall social and economic development. The starting point of reform was rural institutional innovation centered on the "all-around responsibility system." Twenty-eight years since the launch of China's reform and opening-up policy, institutional innovation once again proceeded from rural reform, with one single goal: to achieve the further liberation of China's productive forces.

In addition, China at this time had, on the whole, had already reached the development stage of promoting agriculture through industry and spurring rural development through urban development, and had begun to possess the conditions and ability to enhance support for and protection of agriculture and rural areas. Learning from successful experience both at home and abroad, accelerating the building of a new socialist countryside and achieving the coordinated socio-economic development of urban and rural areas became the essence of China's entire reform and development initiative.

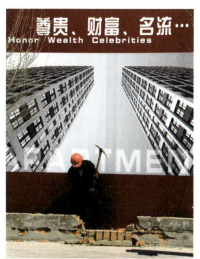

Of course, the fundamental reason was that China's achievements in rural development had mainly benefited from implementation of the household contract responsibility system;

but while efforts towards the gradual realization of public ownership, the establishment of the modern enterprise system and other reforms in China's cities had achieved significant progress since the 1990s, little substantive progress had been made in the institutional innovation of China's rural areas. Although it would be exaggerating to say that the countryside was becoming unknowingly "marginalized" during reforms to establish and improve China's socialist market economic system, it is nonetheless evident that a great imbalance had emerged, one of the main causes of the ever-widening urban-rural gap since the 1990s. The incompleteness of rural factors of production and administrative departments' intensified monopolization of grain purchasing and distribution led to stagnation in agricultural production and rural income growth. During the seven-year period from 1997 to 2003, farmers' per-capita income rose less than 4 percent per year on average, less than one-fifth the growth rate of urban residents' income. Production in major grain-producing areas and the incomes of most rural households remained unchanged or even

declined, and the development of all kinds of social undertakings in rural areas entered a period of low growth.

Therefore, in October 2005, the central government's calls to "build a new socialist countryside" were viewed as a concrete elucidation of integrated urban and rural development and the implementation of the policy of "industry nurturing agriculture and cities supporting rural areas."

According to government policymakers, building a new socialist countryside is an important safeguard to ensure the enhancement

of comprehensive agricultural productivity and the development of modern agriculture. At present, China's basic infrastructure for agricultural production and material/technological conditions are all relatively poor and "extensive farming" practices are also fairly prevalent. China's modern agricultural construction program is designed to lay the foundation and provide a safeguard for the development of modern agriculture. This initiative encompasses several elements, including accelerating the building of a new countryside; enhancing agricultural productivity; strengthening farmland infrastructure; improving soil quality; building irrigation works; promoting improved seed varieties and cultivation methods;

developing agricultural mechanization; cultivating "new-type farmers," who have a good basic education and understand both agricultural techniques and operations management; and enhancing comprehensive agricultural productivity.

Building a new countryside is not only China's fundamental approach to increasing farmers' incomes and invigorating the rural economy, but also an important aspect of building a harmonious society. In order to achieve a harmonious society, China must first build harmonious villages and towns, and make comprehensive improvements in rural education, sanitation, cultural and other facilities.

30. From Regional Revitalization to Coordinated Development

On September 29, 2003, the Political Bureau of the CCCPC approved *Some Opinions on the Implementation of the Strategy for Revitalizing Northeast China and Other Old Industrial Bases* (hereafter "Some Opinions"). With the ambition to build the "fourth pole" of China's economic growth, central government policymakers and key members of the local governments of China's northeastern provinces (Liaoning, Jilin and Heilongjiang) ushered in the launch of the "Northeast Revitalization" initiative.

Thirty years earlier, no one would have imagined that China's mighty northeast would ever require revitalization. Since the inception of the first Five-Year Plan in 1953, Northeast China had always been the country's industrial backbone. The 58 key projects that were successfully implemented during this period not only endowed the northeast with a relatively independent and comprehensive national economic system but, more importantly, enabled the basic elements of the then fashionable planned economic system to take root and spread on the fertile soil of Northeast China.

In late autumn 2003, the second week after the central government passed the resolution to revitalize the northeast, Hong Hu, then governor of Jilin Province, described to journalists the reasons for launching the Northeast Revitalization policy: "The decentralization of administrative powers, an extreme imbalance in China's regional economic development, the independence of each region's market resources and the difficult nature of reasonably allocating these resources through market and administrative means have resulted in an ever-widening gap in regional development and have exacerbated conflicts in social and economic development." The initial intention of policymakers, therefore, was to introduce policies to help transfer the successful experience of China's east-

ern coastal regions to northeastern, central and western, thereby achieving the sequential and rapid development of the country's regional economies.

In November 1999, the strategic decision to develop West China (the "West China Development" initiative) was finalized at the Central Economic Work Conference; and, in March 2004, Premier Wen Jiabao, in his government work report, called explicitly for promotion of the "Rise of Central China" initiative. China's three major economic regions were thus fully encompassed by the West China Development, Northeast Revitalization, and Rise of Central China strategic initiatives.

In May 2007, the State Council's Northeast Revitalization Of-

fice issued an appraisal report stating that, since implementing the Northeast Revitalization strategy, the government's policy, financial and project support had steadily increased and was essentially in place; and that Northeast China's economic development and social progress had achieved positive and gratifying results. However,

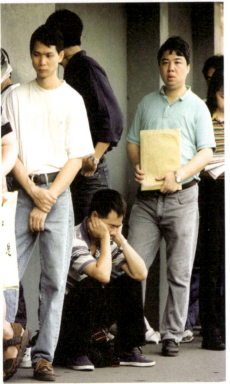

the report also added a reminder: "These results are only an interim step. The disparity between Northeast China and developed regions is still widening; the task of structural adjustment is extremely arduous; the advancement of reform and strategic recombination of state-owned enterprises is fraught with difficulties; sustainable development in the equipment manufacturing industry faces severe challenges; the sustainable development of resource-based cities is not safeguarded by policies; and there is great pressure on employment and social security. Many risks still remain."

Meanwhile, the progress status of the West China Development and Rise of Central China initiatives was similar to that of Northeast Revitalization. It had become evident that the simple replication of East China's developmental path was not the way to success.

The new thinking that emerged was that China's eastern coastal regions and foundationally strong northeast could serve as the main economic propeller for the country's development and competitiveness, that Central China should actively participate in industrial transfer in harmony with its resource environment, and that West China should focus primarily

on resource conservation and environmental protection. In this way, China can shift from the inefficient approach of running multiple "economic machines" simultaneously to the optimized operation of a single, integrated machine with coordinated functions and well-defined roles.

This "functional division" philosophy has redefined and altered the direction of China's regional development. Guided by this ideology and in accordance with each region's resource carrying capacity, current development density, development potential and functional role, China's territory was divided into four categories: optimal development areas, key development areas, restricted development areas, and prohibited development areas. By holistically planning the distribution of productive forces, clearly defin-

ing different directions of development and controlling different development intensities, a regional development pattern—under which population, economy and resource environment are all coordinated—has gradually been formed.

These coordinated roles of development are not only a much more realistic approach, but also better in line with the Scientific Outlook on Development ideology than the uncoordinated and unilateral pursuit of GDP growth by each province and region. After over ten years of unremitting efforts, a development strategy for China's regional economy suited to the country's own conditions was finally found. In March 2008, the State Council Office of the Leading Group for West China Development and the State Council Office of the Leading Group for Revitalizing Northeast China and Other Old Industrial Bases were merged and integrated into the State Development and Reform Commission.

图书在版编目（CIP）数据

改革开放30年最具影响力的30件经济大事：英文／《商务周刊》杂志社 编著；（加）马修·杜鲁门（Trueman, M.）译. —北京：新星出版社，2008.10
ISBN 978-7-80225-541-8

I.改… II.①商…②杜… III.改革开放－大事记－中国－英文 IV.D61

中国版本图书馆CIP数据核字（2008）第162170号

改革开放30年最具影响力的30件经济大事
《商务周刊》杂志社 编著 （加）马修·杜鲁门 译

责任编辑：张维
责任印制：韦舰
内文设计：正美 书籍装帧设计部 010-64003130
封面设计：尧尧

出版发行：新星出版社
出 版 人：谢　刚
社　　址：北京市东城区金宝街67号隆基大厦　100005
网　　址：www.newstarpress.com
电　　话：010-65270477
传　　真：010-65270449
法律顾问：北京建元律师事务所
国际经销：中国国际图书贸易总公司（中国北京车公庄西路35号）
公司地址：北京邮政信箱第399号　100044
印　　刷：北京中科印刷有限公司
开　　本：787×1092　1/16
版　　次：2008年10月第一版
书　　号：ISBN 978-7-80225-541-8